FAVOURITE
MEAT
STEP-BY-STEP
RECIPES

Your Promise of Success

Welcome to the world of Confident C
created for you in the Test Kitchen,
recipes are double tested by our tea
home economists to achieve a high standard
of success and delicious results every time.

D1361342

C O N T E

Braised Oxtail, page 81.

Spinach and Pecan Seasoned Veal, page 19.

Open-faced Focaccia and Piquant Steak, page 33.

Fettuccine Bolognese, page 101.

N T S

Lamb Cutlets with Redcurrant Orange Glaze, page 76.

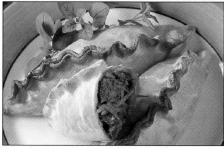
Cornish Pasties, page 102.

The Publisher thanks the following for their assistance in the photography for this book: Waterford Wedgwood; Accoutrement; Sandy de Beyer 'Home at Last'; The Bay Tree; Hale Imports; Fred Pazotti Tiles. All suppliers in Sydney.

We also thank the Australian Meat & Live-Stock Corporation and the Australian Pork Corporation.

Home-style Lamb Pie, page 108.

Lamb Schnitzels, page 74.

The test kitchen where our recipes are double-tested by our team of home economists to achieve a high standard of success and delicious results every time.

When we test our recipes, we rate them for ease of preparation. You will find the following cookery ratings on the recipes in this book, making them easy to use and understand.

A single Cooking with Confidence symbol indicates a recipe that is simple and generally quick to make – perfect for beginners.

Two symbols indicate the need for just a little more care and a little more time.

Three symbols indicate these are special dishes that need more investment in time, care and patience – but the results will be well worth it.

Meat Basics

There are numerous cuts of beef, veal, lamb and pork, each with its own
flavour and cooking qualities. This guide to purchasing, storage, cooking
and presentation will ensure you make the most of each cut.

It is important to select the best meat possible for the recipe you intend to cook. Here is advice on what to look for and how to store your purchase prior to cooking.

Purchasing

At the butcher or supermarket, choose meat cuts that are as lean as possible; there is no point in paying for fat that you will trim off when you get home. A little fat helps keep the meat moist during grilling or barbecuing. Meat for stir-frying must be as lean as possible. There is considerable awareness nowadays among consumers that lean meat is an important part of a well-balanced, nutritionally sound diet. Meat producers and butchers have responded accordingly with leaner cuts that are flavoursome and healthy. Today's beef, veal, lamb and pork are relatively low in fat, kilojoules and cholesterol-producing agents. The various meats are a great source of protein, iron, zinc and other essential nutrients.

Look for meat that has a clear, fresh appearance; meat with a greyish tinge has been poorly handled and stored and must be avoided. An unpleasant odour and slimy surface are other indicators that the product is unacceptable. Offal such as kidneys and liver that have a strong smell of ammonia must also be rejected.

Buy the appropriate cut of meat for the cooking process you will be using. Each cut has distinctive qualities that can be used to advantage in a specific instance. Don't buy a cut more expensive than you need – a cheaper one may well give a better result in your particular recipe. Here is a guide to the cuts used in this book.

Roasting
Beef – Blade, fillet, mince, rib, rib eye, rump, set of ribs, silverside, sirloin, skirt, topside.
Veal – Fillet, leg, loin/eye of loin, rump, shoulder.
Lamb – Chump, eye of loin, forequarter, leg, mid loin, mince, rack/crown roast, shanks, shoulder.
Pork – Boneless loin, cutlets, fillet, foreloin roast, leg, loin medallion steak, mince, shoulder

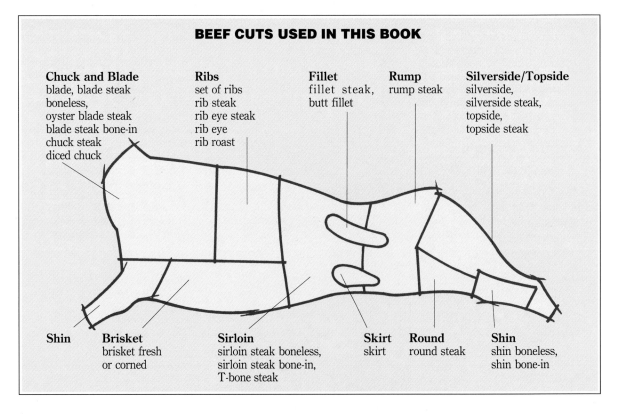

BEEF CUTS USED IN THIS BOOK

Chuck and Blade
blade, blade steak
boneless,
oyster blade steak
blade steak bone-in
chuck steak
diced chuck

Ribs
set of ribs
rib steak
rib eye steak
rib eye
rib roast

Fillet
fillet steak,
butt fillet

Rump
rump steak

Silverside/Topside
silverside,
silverside steak,
topside,
topside steak

Shin

Brisket
brisket fresh
or corned

Sirloin
sirloin steak boneless,
sirloin steak bone-in,
T-bone steak

Skirt
skirt

Round
round steak

Shin
shin boneless,
shin bone-in

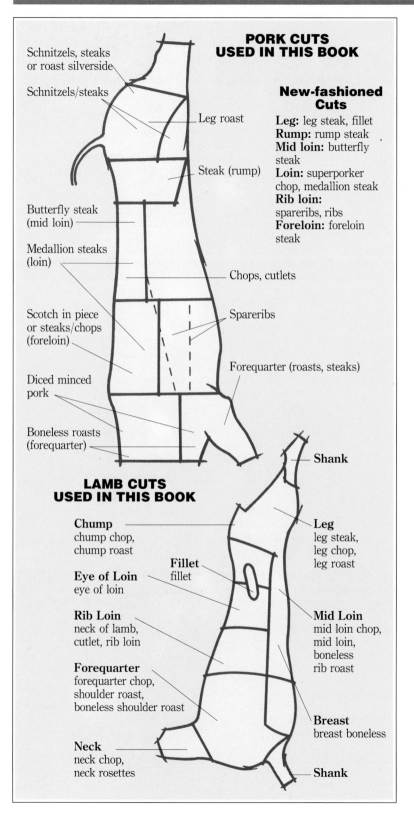

PORK CUTS USED IN THIS BOOK

Schnitzels, steaks or roast silverside

Schnitzels/steaks

Leg roast

Steak (rump)

Butterfly steak (mid loin)

Medallion steaks (loin)

Chops, cutlets

Scotch in piece or steaks/chops (foreloin)

Spareribs

Diced minced pork

Forequarter (roasts, steaks)

Boneless roasts (forequarter)

New-fashioned Cuts

Leg: leg steak, fillet
Rump: rump steak
Mid loin: butterfly steak
Loin: superporker chop, medallion steak
Rib loin: spareribs, ribs
Foreloin: foreloin steak

LAMB CUTS USED IN THIS BOOK

Chump
chump chop, chump roast

Eye of Loin
eye of loin

Rib Loin
neck of lamb, cutlet, rib loin

Forequarter
forequarter chop, shoulder roast, boneless shoulder roast

Neck
neck chop, neck rosettes

Fillet
fillet

Shank

Leg
leg steak, leg chop, leg roast

Mid Loin
mid loin chop, mid loin, boneless rib roast

Breast
breast boneless

Shank

Barbecuing
Beef – Steaks: Blade, fillet, minute steaks, rib, rib eye, rump, sirloin, T-bone. Also, mince and spareribs.
Veal – Chops/cutlets/steaks: Fillet, forequarter, leg, loin, rump, schnitzel, shoulder. Also, eye of loin.
Lamb – Chops/cutlets: Best neck, chump, forequarter, leg, mid loin rib, rib loin, shoulder. Also, eye of loin, fillet, leg steak, mince, noisettes.
Pork – American-style ribs, boneless loin, butterfly steaks, diced pork, forequarter chops, foreloin roast and steak, leg steak, loin chop, loin medallion steak, spareribs.

Grilling
Beef – Steaks: Fillet, minute steak, oyster blade, rib, rib eye, rump, sirloin, T-bone. Also, mince, spareribs.
Veal – Chops/cutlets/steaks: Fillet, forequarter, leg, loin, rump, schnitzel, shoulder. Also eye of loin.
Lamb – Chops/cutlets: Best neck, chump, forequarter, leg, mid loin, rib loin, shoulder. Also, eye of loin, fillet, leg steak, mince, noisettes.
Pork – American-style ribs, butterfly steak, cutlets, diced pork, fillet, foreloin steak, forequarter chops, leg schnitzels, leg steak, loin chops, loin medallion steak, spareribs.

Stir-frying
Beef – Blade, fillet, rib eye, round, rump, sirloin, topside.
Veal – Eye of loin, fillet, leg, rump, shoulder.
Lamb – Eye of loin, fillet, leg, shoulder.
Pork – Diced pork, leg schnitzels, fillet.

Pan-frying
Beef – Steaks: Fillet, minute, oyster blade, rib, rib eye, rump, sirloin, T-bone. Also, mince, spareribs.
Veal – Chops/cutlets/steaks: Fillet, forequarter, leg, loin, rump, schnitzel, shoulder. Also, eye of loin, mince.
Lamb – Chops/cutlets: Best neck, chump, forequarter, leg, mid loin, rib loin, shoulder. Also, eye of loin, fillet, leg steak, mince, noisettes.
Pork – Butterfly steak, forequarter chops, cutlets, fillet, foreloin steak, leg schnitzels, leg steak, loin chops, medallion steak, spareribs. Also mince, diced pork.

Braising
Beef – Bolar blade, brisket, chuck, round, shin, silverside, skirt, spareribs, topside.
Veal – Knuckle/osso bucco, shoulder.
Lamb – Chump, forequarter, leg, mince, neck chops/rosettes, shank, shoulder.
Pork – Forequarter chops, loin medallions, spareribs

Storing

Meat that is frozen or fresh must be transported home as quickly as possible. Do not leave it sitting in the sun in your car or car boot. The internal temperature of a car left closed in full sun spells disaster to all meat products. The longer that food spends at temperatures between 5°C and 60°C, the greater the likelihood of rapid growth of harmful bacteria that may result in food poisoning.

Keep meat away from any strong-smelling items such as cleaning agents and petrol that you may have stored in your vehicle; meat quickly absorbs the smell of things around it. Make it your policy to purchase meat as the last item on your round of shopping. In hot weather, it's a good idea to use an insulated chiller bag to keep it cold.

Cuts of meat that have begun to defrost must not be refrozen; defrost fully in the refrigerator and cook within two days. The cooked item can then, of course, be frozen.

Make sure that cuts of meat from the freezer department of your supermarket are solid – do not purchase any that appear semi-soft and that are sitting in their own drip. Meat that is inadequately packaged and may have been subject to freezer burn should also be rejected.

Storing frozen meat: Once you get your purchase home, ready frozen

Storage of Fresh Meat

Mince and sausages	2 days
Cubed meat	2-3 days
Steaks, chops, cutlets	2-3 days
Roasts (with bone)	3-4 days
Roasts (boned, rolled)	3-4 days
Corned beef	1 week
Vacuum-packed beef	4 weeks

items that you are not intending to cook for days or even weeks, must be placed directly in the freezer. Detailed information on freezing fresh and cooked meat is given on the next page.
Storing fresh meat: Cuts of fresh meat in supermarkets are often sold in disposable trays, covered in plastic wrap. The important thing is to ensure that the meat is not sitting in its own drip; it must also be kept as dry as possible. Remove meat from its packaging, pat dry on absorbent paper and place on a rack in a deep dish (to catch the drip) loosely covered with foil or plastic wrap. Store in the coldest part of the refrigerator (at the top in a refrigerator/freezer unit). If meat is to be cooked within two days, it can be left in its original packaging, providing meat is not wet.

Cold air must be able to circulate freely around the meat; the temperature range should be 0°C to 4°C. Check that you understand the temperature control dial on your refrigerator; some models are misleading and you may be unwittingly increasing the temperature rather than decreasing it.

See the Storage of Fresh Meat guide below for details of how long to store fresh meat in the refrigerator. The more cutting and preparation the meat undergoes, the shorter will be the storage time. This explains why mince has a shorter storage time than steaks, chops or cutlets.

To prevent cross-contamination, do not store cooked and fresh meat near one another. Store cooked meat above raw so that raw cannot drip onto the cooked item.

Meat can be stored in the special meat compartment of the refrigerator. Unwrap the meat and arrange it in the compartment in stacks not more than two to three layers deep. Cover top of meat loosely with foil or waxed paper to prevent the surface drying out.

Never handle cooked and uncooked meats together; bacteria can be transferred from one to the other by cooking utensils and your hands. Wash your hands, scrub chopping boards in very hot water and wash all utensils before changing from working with raw meat to cooked. Remember that tepid, dirty washing up water is also a breeding ground for bacteria.

Leftover cooked meat hot from the

oven must be cooled rapidly in the refrigerator and not left to cool at room temperature. A kitchen is often hot and the perfect environment for unwelcome bacteria to multiply.

Sauces and stuffings will cause stored meat to spoil. Remove stuffing from meat; store meat, stuffing and sauce separately in the refrigerator.

Freezing

Use heavy-gauge polythene bags, sturdy plastic boxes such as ice-cream containers, aluminium trays and good quality plastic wrap. Label all packages with the details of the content (cut and type of meat), its unfrozen weight or number of people it will feed and the date it was packaged and stored. Use a waterproof pen or wax crayon. Once the package becomes an unidentifiable, frozen mass, you'll regret not having labelled it!

If a package has partially defrosted, it must never be refrozen; defrost fully in the refrigerator and cook within the suggested storage time.

Meat purchased on a styrofoam tray should be fully repackaged before freezing; discard the tray.

The freezer should be set at minus 15°C or lower.

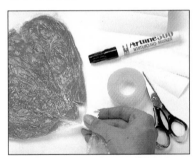

Freezing uncooked meat: Flatten to a thin package. Remove air; tape closed.

Affix label stating contents, weight and date of packaging.

Freezing cooked casserole: Line cake tin with plastic bag; ladle in the meat. Seal.

Place in freezer; when frozen, remove bag from tin, expel air and reseal.

Alternatively, freeze directly in plastic containers or aluminium trays.

To freeze uncooked meat: It is important to expel as much air as possible from the packaging; oxygen left behind will speed up the process of oxidisation of any fat, resulting in an unpleasant taste after prolonged storage. If you do a lot of freezing, it is worth investing in a vacuum freezer pump to efficiently expel the air.

Secure freezer bags by twisting the tops and closing them with masking tape; this is preferable to metal twist ties. Or, clip a metal band in place using a clipping device.

As a general rule, uncooked meat can be frozen for up to six months. Liver and kidneys do not freeze well and are better purchased when needed.

Steaks and chops: Wrap individually in plastic wrap, expelling air. Pad bones with aluminium foil to prevent wrap tearing. Pack the number required in a high-density plastic bag; extract air, twist top and seal with tape. Label and freeze.

Mince and boneless cuts for stewing and braising: Cut meat into strips or cubes. Weigh out meal-sized portions and place in heavy-gauge plastic bags and fill right into the corners with meat. Flatten the package as much as possible (so it will defrost evenly and quickly). Expel air, twist top, seal with tape. Label and freeze.

Roasting joints and corned meats: Place meat in a heavy-gauge plastic bag; expel as much air as possible – a vacuum pump is preferable in this instance. Tape end of bag to package. Label and freeze.

To freeze cooked meat: Quickly reduce the temperature of the cooked item by placing it in the refrigerator or by plunging the base of the dish into cold water. Then cool completely in the refrigerator.

Do not freeze roasted joints of meat because the freezing process robs them of flavour and moisture. Sliced roast meats covered with gravy can, however, be frozen successfully but must be reheated gently or they will become tough and stringy.

Curries, stews, casseroles, soups, meatballs and meat sauces for pasta are all suitable for freezing. Line cake tins or other suitable containers with heavy-gauge plastic bags. Ladle a sufficient amount of the food into the bag (an individual portion or enough for a meal for several people). Seal each bag and label. Place bag in its tin in the freezer. When frozen, remove from tin, reseal to remove as much air as possible and return, labelled, to the freezer. Alternatively, spoon the meat directly into plastic or aluminium containers. Seal, label and freeze. As a general rule, freeze for a maximum of two months. See Cook's File storage details at the end of each recipe in this book to determine if the dish is suitable for freezing.

Defrosting

Thaw frozen food in the refrigerator or use the defrost setting on your microwave oven (see chart below). Never thaw frozen meat at room temperature. Never keep perishable food at room temperature for longer than two hours – particularly on hot days. This includes time to prepare, serve and eat.

MICROWAVE DEFROSTING CHART

To defrost in a microwave use "defrost" setting, allowing approximately 5 minutes per serve. Always remove meat from wrapping before defrosting. Stir casseroles occasionally to distribute heat evenly. (A casserole serving 6 should take 30 minutes to defrost.) With mince and cubed meat, remove outer sections as they soften to prevent cooking. Separate chops as they defrost. Turn large joints over halfway through defrosting and then let stand for 20-30 minutes before cooking. Stand pork fillet for 10 minutes after defrosting.

Cut	Mins per 500 g	Cut	Mins per 500 g
LAMB			
Large joints	10-14	Chops	6-7
Small joints	7-10	Mince	6-7
BEEF			
Large joints	10-14	Steaks	7-10
Small joints	8-10	Mince	7-10
VEAL			
Large joints	10-14	Chops	7-10
Small joints	8-10	Diced veal, mince	7-10
PORK			
Roasts	7-8	Chops	5-6
Fillet	8-10		

Cooking Techniques

There are two cooking methods, using either dry heat or moist heat.

Dry heat cookery comprises oven roasting, barbecuing and grilling, stir-frying and pan-frying. Tender cuts of meat are ideal. Timing is crucial to prevent a tough, dry result.

Moist heat cookery comprises braising, casseroling and pot roasting. The less tender cuts are ideal here because they benefit from the long, slow cooking times.

There are some general principles to observe for each of the cooking methods used in this book. Whatever method you are using, when testing meat to see how well it is cooked, simply press it with blunt tongs. Cutting the meat allows the escape of precious juices which keep the meat moist and tender. Similarly, turn meat with tongs, not with a fork.

Roasting: Weigh meat so that you can calculate the correct roasting time. The chart below is a general guide to roasting. When meats are boned

To roast, place meat thermometer in the thickest part of the roast.

Gauge indicates the degree to which the roast has cooked.

and/or stuffed, cooking times and temperatures will vary – refer to individual recipes.

If preferred, a meat thermometer can be used to indicate the degree of doneness. Insert the thermometer into the thickest part of the meat, away from fat or bone, to ensure accurate temperature readings. Meat thermometers are available from specialty kitchen shops.

Barbecuing: Cooking times will depend on the thickness of the meat, the efficiency of the barbecue and your taste. To test for doneness, press with blunt tongs. Springy indicates that the meat is rare; slightly resistant indicates medium and firm to the touch signifies well done.

Give the barbecue plenty of time to heat so that the meat is cooking over glowing coals, not over flames.

When barbecuing kebabs, oiled metal skewers are ideal because it is easier to remove the cooked meat from them. Soak bamboo or wooden skewers in water for about 30 minutes to prevent scorching, or cover ends with aluminium foil.

Marinades add flavour and help to tenderise tougher cuts of meat. Leave meat in the marinade, covered, in the refrigerator for at least two hours, preferably overnight. Use honey or sugar sparingly in marinades as sweet mixtures easily scorch.

Grilling: Many of the rules for barbecuing can be applied to grilling.

Thin cuts of meat need to be nicked around the edges to prevent curling.

Drain marinated meat thoroughly before grilling to reduce steam during cooking and ensure a tender result.

If your grill pan is lined with foil, puncture a few holes to allow fat to drain away. Ideally, place meat on a

ROASTING TIMES AND INTERNAL TEMPERATURES

Note: Not all beef and lamb cuts are calculated the same way because of their variation in size.

Beef Eye Fillet – Roast at Moderately Hot 210°C	
Rare	15-20 minutes/500 g (60°C internal temp)
Medium	20-25 minutes/500 g (70°C internal temp)
Well done	25-30 minutes/500 g (75°C internal temp)
Lamb Neck Fillet, Eye of Loin, Boneless Chump, Topside Roast, Round Roast – Roast at Moderately Hot 210°C	
Medium	9-10 minutes/100 g (70°C internal temp)
Well done	11-12 minutes/100 g (75°C internal temp)
Lamb Rack and Crown Roast– Roast at Moderately Hot 210°C	
Medium-well done	Total 45-55 minutes, irrespective of weight.
All other beef and lamb cuts except the above – Roast at Moderate 180°C	
Rare	20-25 minutes/500 g (60°C internal temp)
Medium	25-30 minutes/500 g (70°C internal temp)
Well done	30-35 minutes/500 g (75°C internal temp)
Pork Leg Roast – Roast at Moderate 180°C	
With bone	30 minutes/500 g (76°C internal temp)
Boneless	23 minutes/500 g (76°C internal temp)
Pork Loin Roast – Roast at Moderate 180°C	
With Bone	30 minutes/500 g (76°C internal temp)
Boneless	30 minutes/500 g (76°C internal temp)

To grill or barbecue, cover ends of skewers with foil to prevent scorching.

To braise, brown meat well to seal in the flavour and juices.

cold, lightly-oiled grill and cook under high heat for the specified number of minutes each side to seal, turning once. For a rare result, cook a further minute each side. Then lower grill tray or reduce heat and continue cooking for the stated amount of time for medium and well done results. Brush or baste with reserved marinade several times during cooking.

Pan-frying: Heat oil or butter in heavy-based pan on high heat, add meat and cook 2-3 minutes each side to seal in juices. Depending on thickness of meat, for a rare result, remove at this stage (meat should be springy to touch). Reduce heat to medium. For a medium result cook for 4-6 minutes

To pan-fry, trim meat of excess fat and sinew before cooking.

Cook over high heat until browned, reduce heat and cook, turning once.

total each side. For well-done meat, cook for 8-12 minutes total each side.

Turn meat once only during cooking and leave pan uncovered. Too low a heat, turning too often, or covering the pan will make the meat tough.

Always drain marinated meat thoroughly before pan-frying.

Braising: To prepare meat, trim excess fat and sinew. Heat oil in a heavy-based pan and quickly brown the meat to seal in juices. (Cook cubed meat, chops, etc, in small batches.)

Add the other ingredients, bring quickly to simmering point, reduce heat and simmer on low to ensure a moist, tender result – small bubbles should gently break the surface. Boiling will make meat tough.

Stir-frying: This rapid method of cooking uses strips of meat, trimmed of all fat and sinew. Meat must be cut evenly so that it cooks at an even rate.

Heat a little oil in a wok or large heavy-based frying pan. Stir-fry by tossing meat quickly in small batches over high heat until cooked.

To stir-fry, cut meat across the grain into even strips.

Stir-fry meat strips over high heat, tossing quickly until cooked.

Sharpening Knives

Steel method: Place edge of knife blade near the top of the steel at a 20° angle. Quickly bring knife down and across the steel until the tip touches the bottom. Repeat on the opposite side of steel. Six strokes on each side are usually enough to get a good sharp edge. Make the last strokes very light.

Wet Stone method: Using gentle pressure, hold the knife blade at a 20° angle to stone. Pass the knife along its entire length. Turn knife over, repeat until knife is sharp.

Basic rules for carving

Allow roast meats to sit for 15 minutes, covered loosely with foil, before carving. Use a good-quality knife, as sharp as possible (see previous page for sharpening instructions). A carving board to carve meat will avoid scratches on serving platters or dulling the knife. Carve meat across the grain, with a slicing rather than sawing action, making use of the full length of the carving-knife blade and with light pressure to avoid tearing the meat.

Carving standing beef rib roast

Carving is easier if you have the backbone removed by the butcher and the rib bones cut short. Usually a rib roast is carved into slices, but hearty eaters may like a whole rib. Place the roast on a platter with rib side down and bone ends to the left. Using tip of knife, release meat from bone. Slice meat parallel to bone from top to rib. Using tip of knife cut along the bone, keeping close to bone, to release slices.

Carving beef fillet

Present the beef fillet at the table on a warmed serving platter, if desired. Use a fork and the flat of the carving-knife blade to transfer it to the carving board, holding the fillet in place with the back of the fork. (Try not to pierce the meat.) Begin slicing at the wide end of the fillet, keeping the blade of the knife slightly tilted and carving across the grain. Make the slices about 2 cm thick. To keep the warmth and juices within the slices, stack them closely together to one side of the carving board. Serve immediately.

Carving ham

Place the ham on cutting board with bone to the left. Insert the fork firmly and carve a slice from underneath to allow the ham to sit flat. Remove slice with tongs. Using a clean cloth, hold the leg firmly and slice into the meat about 10 cm from the knuckle.

Make another cut at an angle to the first and remove the wedge of ham. Make several thin slices right down to the bone. To release the slices, run knife along the bone. Lift off slices on the flat of the knife and arrange attractively on a serving platter.

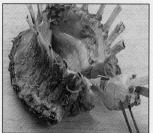

Carving crown of lamb

If the cavity has been stuffed, transfer the stuffing to a warm serving platter prior to carving. To carve, place the roast on carving board. Steady the roast with a carving fork and slice downward between each pair of ribs. To ensure even slices, keep close to the bone, always to the right or left. Remove one chop at a time. As a general rule there are two chops per serving, plus stuffing.

Carving leg of lamb

Place the roasted leg of lamb on the carving board. Insert the fork firmly on the left side. Remove two or three slices from the underside, cutting lengthways. Turn the roast so that it rests on the cut surface, which forms a secure base. Starting at the opposite end to the shank, make parallel slices down to the bone. Either make one or two slices at a time, cutting across the bottom with the tip of the knife to release them, or slice all the way along the full length of the leg bone and then release the slices all at once by cutting under them, keeping the knife close to the bone. To carve the tasty collar of meat closer to the shank, slice the meat towards the shank giving even slices, cutting across the grain. Turn the leg of lamb over to carve the other side, making parallel slices as before. Place the slices of lamb onto warmed plates or a warmed serving platter as you cut them, to retain heat. Serve immediately.

Carving rack of lamb

Place the rack of rib chops on the carving board, with the bones facing away from you. To steady the rack while you carve, lightly pierce the meat with the fork at the left end, holding with the knife. Make the first cut after the first rib. If the first chop is very small make the first cut between the second and third rib bones and serve the first two ribs as one chop. Cut the remaining ribs one at a time, being careful to cut straight down and not at an angle or you will have three bones and no meat when you reach the end. To serve, pick up the chop on the flat of the knife, holding it firmly with the carving fork.

ROASTS

ROAST BEEF WITH RED WINE SAUCE AND YORKSHIRE PUDDINGS

Preparation time: 20 minutes
Cooking time: 1 hour 15 minutes
   to 2 hours + 2 hours marinating
Serves 8

1 cup red wine
2 bay leaves
1 medium onion, finely chopped
4 whole cloves
1 teaspoon cracked black
   peppercorns
1 x 2.5 kg boneless rib roast
2/3 cup water
1/2 cup plum conserve
2 chicken stock cubes,
   crumbled
1 tablespoon cornflour
1/3 cup water

Never-fail Yorkshire Puddings
1/3 cup olive oil
2 cups self-raising flour
2 eggs, lightly beaten
1½ cups milk

➤ PLACE WINE, bay leaves, onion, cloves and peppercorns in a large dish; stir to combine. Add meat, turning to coat with marinade. Store in refrigerator, covered with plastic wrap, for 2 hours or overnight; turn meat occasionally. Drain meat, reserving marinade.

1 Preheat oven to moderately hot 210°C. Place meat on a roasting rack in a deep baking dish; pour the water in the bottom.

Roast meat for 1 hour 15 minutes for a rare result, 1 hour 40 minutes for medium result and 2 hours for well done. Baste the meat occasionally with the reserved marinade. Remove from oven. Leave in warm place 10 minutes, covered with foil, before slicing.

2 Combine the juices in pan with the reserved marinade, conserve and stock cubes. Stir over low heat until mixture boils. Blend cornflour with water to make a smooth paste. Add to the mixture in the pan, stir over medium heat 3 minutes or until sauce boils and thickens; strain. Serve separately.

3 **To make Yorkshire Puddings:** Preheat the oven to hot 240°C. Place a teaspoon of the oil in the base of each of 2 x 6 cup deep muffin tins. Place in oven 10 minutes.

Sift flour in a medium mixing bowl; make a well in the centre. Add combined eggs and milk all at once. Beat until all liquid is incorporated and the batter is free of lumps. Half-fill each of the hot muffin tins with batter. Bake for 15 minutes or until well risen and golden. Makes 12.

COOK'S FILE

Storage time: Leftover beef can be stored in the refrigerator for 2 days. Any covered with gravy must be discarded. Store remaining gravy separately.
Variation: Lard can be used in place of olive oil for the Yorkshire Puddings; this gives a good colour and flavour.

BEEF WELLINGTON

Preparation time: 5 minutes
Cooking time: 45 minutes
  to 1 hour 30 minutes
Serves 6 to 8

1 kg beef fillet or rib eye
  in one piece
freshly ground black pepper
1 tablespoon oil
2 tablespoons brandy
125 g peppercorn pâté
60 g button mushrooms,
  sliced
2 sheets frozen puff pastry,
  thawed
1 egg, lightly beaten

➤ PREHEAT OVEN to moderately hot 210°C. Trim meat of excess fat and sinew. Fold tail end under. Tie meat securely with string at regular intervals.
1 Rub meat with pepper. Heat oil in a large, heavy-based pan. Add meat and cook over a high heat, browning well all over. Remove from heat.
Add the brandy and ignite carefully, using a long match or taper. Shake pan until flames subside. Leave meat to cool.
2 Spread pâté over top and sides of beef. Cover with mushrooms, pressing them onto the pâté.
Place pastry sheets on a lightly floured surface. Brush one edge with a little egg and overlap the edge of the other sheet, pressing well to join.
3 Place the beef on the pastry, folding pastry over to enclose the meat completely; trim excess pastry and use to decorate the top, if desired. Brush edges with egg and seal. Cut a few slits in the top to allow the steam to escape. Brush the top and sides with egg. Transfer to a baking dish and cook for 45 minutes for a rare result,

1 hour for medium result and 1 hour 30 minutes for well done. Remove from oven. Leave in a warm place for 10 minutes, lightly covered with foil. Slice and serve.

1

2

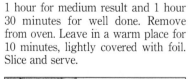

3

ROAST BEEF FILLET WITH EASY BÉARNAISE SAUCE

Preparation time: 10 minutes
Cooking time: 45 minutes
  to 1 hour 10 minutes
Serves 6

1 x 1.5 kg whole beef fillet
freshly ground black pepper, to
  taste
1 tablespoon oil
30 g butter
1 clove garlic, crushed
1 cup water

Easy Béarnaise Sauce
½ cup tarragon vinegar
2 bay leaves
2 teaspoons black
  peppercorns

4 spring onions, chopped
5 egg yolks, lightly beaten
250 g butter, melted

➤ PREHEAT OVEN to moderately hot 210°C. Trim the meat of excess fat and sinew.

1 Tie meat securely with string at regular intervals to retain its shape. Rub meat all over with pepper.

2 Heat oil, butter and garlic in a deep baking dish on top of the stove, add meat; brown it all over on high heat. Place a rack in the dish and put the meat on top; add the water to dish. Transfer to oven.
Roast meat for 45 minutes for a rare result, 1 hour for a medium result and 1 hour 10 minutes for well done. Baste the meat occasionally with the pan juices. Remove from oven. Leave in a warm place for 10 minutes, covered with foil. Remove string before slicing.

3 To make Easy Béarnaise Sauce: Combine vinegar, bay leaves, peppercorns and spring onion in small pan. Bring to boil, reduce heat to a simmer, cook, uncovered, until liquid has reduced to 2 tablespoons. Strain, reserving the liquid.
Place liquid and egg yolks in a food processor bowl or blender, process for 30 seconds. With motor constantly running, add melted butter slowly in a thin stream, processing until it is all added. Serve with the sliced meat.

COOK'S FILE

Storage time: Leftover meat can be stored in the refrigerator for 2 days. Bring to room temperature before serving. Easy Béarnaise Sauce can be prepared up to the stage of adding the melted butter, several hours in advance. Add the butter just before the meat is sliced and served.

1

2

3

STANDING RIB ROAST WITH HORSERADISH CREAM

Preparation time: 10 minutes
Cooking time: 1 hour
   to 1 hour 30 minutes
Serves 8 to 10

1 x 1.5 kg standing rib roast
1 tablespoon oil
2 cloves garlic, crushed
freshly ground black pepper

Horseradish Cream
3 egg yolks, lightly beaten
3 tablespoons horseradish
   relish
1 teaspoon white vinegar

½ teaspoon mustard powder
freshly ground black pepper, to
   taste
1 cup light olive oil

➤ PREHEAT OVEN to hot 240°C.
Trim meat of excess fat and sinew.
1 Tie meat securely with string at regular intervals to retain its shape. Rub all over with the combined oil, garlic and pepper; place in a deep baking dish, bone side down (which forms a natural rack).
2 Roast meat for 15 minutes. Reduce heat to moderate 180°C. Cook further 45 minutes for rare, 1 hour for medium and 1 hour 15 minutes for well done. Baste meat occasionally with pan juices. Remove from oven. Leave in a warm place 10 minutes,

covered with foil. Remove the string. To carve, cut close along the bones and remove fillet; then slice vertically. Serve with Horseradish Cream.
3 To make Horseradish Cream: Place the egg yolks, relish, vinegar, mustard and pepper in a food processor bowl or blender. With the motor running constantly, add the oil slowly in a thin, steady stream until it has all been added and the mixture is thick and pale.

COOK'S FILE

Storage time: Cook this dish just before serving. Leftover meat can be stored in the refrigerator for 2 days. Horseradish Cream can be made 1 day ahead and stored in an airtight jar in the refrigerator.

TOPSIDE ROAST

Preparation time: 10 minutes
Cooking time: 40 minutes
   to 1 hour
Serves 6

1 x 1 kg piece topside beef
12 leaves spinach
2 spring onions, finely
   chopped
40 g butter
200 g blue vein cheese

freshly ground black pepper
1 tablespoon oil

➤ PREHEAT OVEN to moderately hot 210°C. Trim meat of excess fat and sinew.
1 Cut a deep pocket in one side.
2 Chop spinach finely, combine with spring onion. Heat butter in pan and cook spinach and spring onion until spinach wilts. Remove from heat; cool. Crumble cheese; mix into spinach; add pepper. Fill pocket with spinach mixture. Close the opening by securing it

with skewers or tying it with string.
3 Heat oil in deep baking dish on top of stove; add meat, brown all over on high heat. Transfer dish to oven. Roast meat 40 minutes for a rare result, 50 minutes for medium, 1 hour for well done. Baste occasionally with pan juices. Remove from oven. Leave in a warm place 10 minutes, covered with foil. Remove string before slicing.

COOK'S FILE

Storage time: Leftover meat can be stored for 2 days in the refrigerator.

Standing Rib Roast with Horseradish Cream (top),
Topside Roast (bottom).

PEPPERED BEEF FILLET WITH GREEN PEPPERCORN SAUCE

Preparation time: 10 minutes
Cooking time: 45 minutes
  to 1 hour 30 minutes
Serves 6

1 x 1 kg whole beef fillet or
  rib eye in one piece
1 tablespoon soy sauce
2 tablespoons freshly cracked
  black peppercorns
3 tablespoons olive oil

Green Peppercorn Sauce
1/2 cup chicken stock
1/2 cup cream
2 teaspoons canned green
  peppercorns, rinsed
  and drained
2 teaspoons brandy

➤ PREHEAT OVEN to moderately
hot 210°C. Tie meat securely with
string at regular intervals to retain its
shape during cooking.

1 Rub meat all over with soy sauce;
roll meat in pepper, pressing to coat
surface and ends.

2 Heat oil in deep baking dish on top
of stove; add meat and brown all over
on high heat. Transfer dish to oven.

3 Roast meat 45 minutes for a rare
result, 1 hour for a medium result and
1 hour 30 minutes for well done. Baste
the meat occasionally with pan juices.
Remove from oven. Leave in a warm
place for 10 minutes, covered with foil.
Remove string before slicing. Serve
with Green Peppercorn Sauce.

**4 To make Green Peppercorn
Sauce:** Add chicken stock to juices in
baking dish. Stir over low heat on top
of stove until boiling; add cream and
peppercorns. Boil 2 minutes, stirring
constantly; add brandy. Boil a further
1 minute; remove from heat.

COOK'S FILE

Storage time: Cook this dish just
before serving. Leftover meat can be
stored in the refrigerator for 2 days.
Discard any beef with sauce over it.
Variation: Stir 1 to 2 tablespoons of
a seeded or smooth, full-flavoured
mustard into the sauce in place of the
green peppercorns.

1

2

3

4

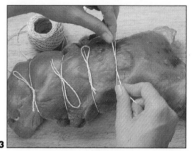

SPINACH AND PECAN SEASONED VEAL

Preparation time: 20 minutes
Cooking time: 1 hour 15 minutes
Serves 6

1 x 1.5 kg boned shoulder
  of veal
2 tablespoons lemon juice
1 tablespoon soy sauce
½ cup chicken stock
¼ cup wine
20 g butter, melted

Spinach and Pecan Seasoning
40 g butter
1 small onion, finely
  chopped
250 g packet frozen, chopped
  spinach
2 tablespoons chopped pecan
  nuts
2 teaspoons currants

➤ PREHEAT OVEN to hot 240°C.
1 Using a sharp knife, cut 1 cm into
and along the thickest part of the veal.
Continue to cut and unroll veal until it
can be opened flat.
2 Spread cooled Spinach and Pecan
Seasoning evenly over meat.
3 Roll and tie meat securely with
string at regular intervals to retain its
shape. Place veal in deep baking dish.
Pour combined juice, sauce, stock,
wine and butter over. Roast meat for
30 minutes. Reduce heat to moderate
180°C, cook 15 minutes more.
4 Baste occasionally with pan juices.
Remove from oven. Leave in warm
place for 10 minutes, covered with foil.
Remove string before slicing.
Heat juices in pan on top of stove over
high heat; bring to boil. Boil for 10
minutes, stirring constantly or until
juices have reduced by half. Season;
strain. Serve over sliced veal.
**To make Spinach and Pecan
Seasoning:** Heat the butter in a small

pan; add the onion, stir over low heat for
5 minutes or until soft.
Add frozen spinach, stir for 10 minutes
over a low heat or until spinach has
thawed and almost all liquid has
evaporated; mixture should be thick.
Remove from heat; season to taste,
cool. Stir in nuts and currants.

COOK'S FILE

Storage time: Cook this dish just
before serving.

CROWN ROAST OF LAMB WITH SAGE STUFFING

Preparation time: 20 minutes
Cooking time: 45 minutes
Serves 6

1 crown roast (minimum
    12 cutlets)
2 medium brown onions, peeled
    and chopped
1 green or cooking apple,
    peeled and chopped
20 g butter
2 cups/about 120 g fresh
    breadcrumbs
2 tablespoons chopped fresh
    sage
1 tablespoon chopped fresh
    parsley
1/4 cup unsweetened apple juice
2 eggs, separated

➤ PREHEAT OVEN to moderately hot 210°C. Trim the meat of excess fat and sinew.

1 Cook onion and apple in butter until soft. Remove from heat and stir in breadcrumbs and herbs. Whisk apple juice and egg yolks together. Stir into breadcrumb mixture.

2 Place egg whites in a small, dry mixing bowl. Using electric beaters, beat egg whites until soft peaks form. Fold lightly into stuffing mixture.

3 Place crown roast in a baking dish. Place a sheet of lightly greased foil in the base of the roast to hold stuffing mixture. Spoon stuffing into the foil cavity. Roast meat for 45 minutes, or until cooked to the degree you like. To serve, cut between cutlets to separate.

COOK'S FILE

Storage time: Cook this dish just before serving.

Hint: Ask your butcher to shape the crown roast and tie it with string. Wrap foil around the cutlet bones to prevent them burning.

1

2

3

ROAST LAMB WITH MINT SAUCE

Preparation time: 20 minutes
Cooking time: 1 hour to 1 hour
    30 minutes
Serves 8

1 x 1.5 kg leg lamb
4 cloves garlic, cut in slivers
1 tablespoon olive oil
½ teaspoon ground black
    pepper
⅔ cup water

Gravy
2 tablespoons plain flour
2 cups chicken stock
2 teaspoons soy sauce

Mint Sauce
¼ cup water
⅓ cup sugar
2 tablespoons malt vinegar
⅓ cup finely chopped fresh
    mint

➤ PREHEAT OVEN to moderately hot 210°C. Trim lamb of excess fat and sinew.

1 Using a sharp knife, make 4 deep slits in the lamb. Insert slivers of garlic in the slits.
Rub meat all over with oil and pepper; place on a roasting rack in deep baking dish; pour the water into dish.

2 Roast meat 1 hour for a rare result, 1 hour 15 minutes for medium result and 1 hour 30 minutes for well done. Baste meat occasionally with pan juices. Remove from oven. Leave in a warm place for 10 minutes, covered with foil. Serve lamb with Gravy and Mint Sauce and commercially made mint jelly, if desired.

3 To make Gravy: Heat pan juices in baking dish; add flour. Stir over a low heat for 3 minutes or until the flour mixture is bubbling and lightly golden. Add combined stock and soy sauce gradually to pan, stirring constantly until gravy boils and thickens. Boil further 1 minute; remove from heat, strain into a jug.

To make Mint Sauce: Combine water and sugar in a small pan. Stir constantly over low heat until mixture boils and sugar has dissolved.

Reduce heat to a simmer, cook mixture without stirring, uncovered, 3 minutes to make a syrup. Remove pan from heat; combine syrup with mint and vinegar in a jug.

COOK'S FILE

Storage time: Leftover lamb can be stored, covered, in the refrigerator, for up to 2 days. Discard any meat that has gravy on it.

ROAST LEG OF LAMB WITH LEEK AND PARSLEY SEASONING

Preparation time: 10 minutes
Cooking time: 1 hour to 1 hour
   45 minutes
Serves 6

1 x 1.8 kg leg of lamb, tunnel
   boned
30 g butter
1 large leek, white part only,
   finely chopped
2 cloves garlic, crushed
1 cup roughly chopped fresh
   parsley
½ cup cream
1½ cups chicken stock

➤ PREHEAT OVEN to moderate 180°C. Trim meat of excess fat and sinew.

1 Heat butter in pan, add leek and garlic, stir over medium heat until soft. Add the parsley and cream. Cook, stirring occasionally, for 5 minutes or until the liquid has evaporated. Leave to cool.

2 Spoon the mixture into the meat. Tuck in ends of meat to enclose mixture, tie meat securely with string to retain its shape during cooking. Place in deep baking dish, add stock.

3 Roast meat for 1 hour for a rare result, 1 hour 15 minutes for medium and 1 hour 45 minutes for well done. Baste the meat occasionally with pan juices. Remove from oven. Leave in a warm place for 10 minutes, covered with foil. Remove string before slicing. Strain pan juices into a jug, serve with the sliced meat.

COOK'S FILE

Storage time: Cook this dish just before serving.

Hint: Ask your butcher to tunnel bone the leg of lamb for you; tunnel boning ensures that the stuffing is securely enclosed during cooking.

Meat is easier to slice if it is left a few minutes in a warm place after cooking.

1

2

3

ORIENTAL RACKS OF LAMB

Preparation time: 15 minutes
Cooking time: 45 to 55 minutes
Serves 4

4 racks of lamb with 4 cutlets
  in each
30 g butter
4 spring onions, chopped
2 cloves garlic, crushed
1 tablespoon chopped fresh
  rosemary
1 cup/60 g fresh white
  breadcrumbs
¼ cup lemon juice
¼ cup honey
1 tablespoon soy sauce
1 cup chicken stock

➤ PREHEAT OVEN to moderately
hot 210°C.

Trim the meat of excess fat and sinew.
1 Cut a pocket in each rack between
the meat and the bone.
2 Heat butter in pan, add spring onion,
garlic and rosemary, stir over medium
heat 3 minutes. Remove from heat, add
breadcrumbs, stir until combined.
Spoon mixture into pockets in meat.
Wrap the bone ends of the racks in foil
to prevent them burning during cooking. Place meat in a deep baking dish.
3 Combine lemon juice, honey and soy
sauce, brush over meat. Roast 45 minutes for a rare result, 50 minutes for
medium and 55 minutes for well done.
4 Baste occasionally with the honey
mixture. Remove from oven. Leave in a
warm place 10 minutes, covered with
foil. Meanwhile, transfer baking dish to
top of stove. Add stock to pan juices.
Bring to boil, reduce to a simmer, cook,
uncovered, 5 minutes or until liquid has
reduced and slightly thickened. Slice the
meat, serve with pan juices.

COOK'S FILE

Storage time: Leftover meat can be
stored, covered, in the refrigerator, for
2 days.
Hint: Heating honey in the microwave
oven for 20 seconds makes it easier to
measure and combine with other
ingredients. If you don't have a
microwave oven, simply stand the jar
in warm water to soften the honey and
make it more workable.

ROAST LAMB WITH ASPARAGUS AND PARMESAN FILLING

Preparation time: 20 minutes
Cooking time: 50 minutes to
  1 hour 10 minutes
Serves 4

1 x 2 kg boned shoulder of lamb
30 g butter
2 tablespoons oil
½ cup white wine
½ cup chicken stock

Asparagus and Parmesan Filling
100 g asparagus spears, cut
  into 1 cm pieces
15 g butter
1 small onion, finely chopped
3 slices prosciutto, finely
  chopped
½ cup/about 30 g fresh white
  breadcrumbs
3 tablespoons freshly grated
  Parmesan cheese
1 egg, lightly beaten

➤ PREHEAT OVEN to moderate 180°C. Trim meat of excess fat and sinew.

1 To make the Asparagus and Parmesan Filling: Cook asparagus in boiling water for 3 minutes or until tender. Drain, rinse under cold water. Heat butter in pan, add onion, stir over low heat until soft. Add prosciutto, stir until brown; remove from heat. Add the breadcrumbs, cheese, egg and asparagus; stir until combined.

2 Open meat out flat, fat side down. Press Filling over meat. Roll up firmly, tucking in edges; tie meat securely with string at regular intervals to retain its shape.

3 Heat butter and oil in deep baking

dish on top of stove; add meat, brown meat all over on high heat. Add wine and stock, transfer dish to oven.

Roast meat 50 minutes for rare result, 1 hour for medium result and 1 hour 10 minutes for well done. Baste meat occasionally with pan juices. Remove from oven. Leave in a warm place for 10 minutes, covered with foil. Remove string before slicing. Strain pan juices, pour over meat to serve.

COOK'S FILE

Storage time: Cook this dish just before serving. Leftover meat can be stored, covered, in the refrigerator for 2 days. Store meat and filling separately.
Variation: Use ham in the Filling in place of prosciutto and vary the type of cheeese used to suit your taste.
Hint: Do not use canned asparagus in this recipe.

ROAST LOIN OF LAMB

Preparation time: 15 minutes
Cooking time: 40 minutes to 1 hour
    15 minutes
Serves 6

2 x 500 g boned lamb loins
¾ cup/about 45 g fresh
    breadcrumbs
¼ cup dry white wine
3 cloves garlic, crushed
¼ cup chopped parsley
1 egg, beaten
200 g pork and veal mince
2 rashers bacon, finely
    chopped

freshly ground black pepper, to
    taste for stuffing
1 teaspoon dried thyme
freshly ground black pepper,
    extra
2 tablespoons oil

➤ PREHEAT OVEN to moderately
slow 160°C. Trim meat of excess fat
and sinew.

1 Place breadcrumbs in a small
mixing bowl; pour wine over. When
breadcrumbs have absorbed the liquid,
add garlic, parsley, egg, mince, bacon,
pepper and thyme. Mix well.

2 Open out loins and spread stuffing
over the inside of lamb. Roll up the
loins; tie them securely with string at

regular intervals to retain their shape.

3 Rub skin of loins with pepper. Heat
oil in deep baking dish on top of stove;
add meat, brown all over on a high
heat. Transfer dish to oven.

Roast meat 40 minutes for a rare result,
1 hour for medium, 1 hour 15 minutes
for well done. Baste meat occasionally
with pan juices. Remove from oven.
Leave in a warm place 10 minutes,
covered with foil. Remove string, slice.

COOK'S FILE

Storage time: Cook this dish just
before serving.

Hint: You may have to order boned
loins of lamb from your butcher in
advance. Ask for them not to be tied.

1

2

3

ROAST PORK LOIN WITH APPLE AND FIGS

Preparation time: 30 minutes
Cooking time: 1 hour 45 minutes
    to 2 hours
Serves 6

1 x 2 kg loin of pork, boned,
    rind removed
125 g pork and veal mince
1 small green apple, peeled,
    chopped
6 dried figs, chopped
½ cup fresh white breadcrumbs
4 spring onions, chopped
2 teaspoons canned, drained,
    chopped green peppercorns

Cider Sauce
2 cups cider
2 cups chicken stock
30 g butter
1 medium onion, thinly sliced
2 cloves garlic, crushed
1 tablespoon plain flour
2 teaspoons French mustard
1 teaspoon Worcestershire
    sauce

➤ PREHEAT OVEN to moderate
180°C. Trim the meat of excess fat
and sinew. Combine the mince, apple,
figs, breadcrumbs, spring onions and
peppercorns.
1 Open meat out flat, spread evenly
with mince mixture, roll up firmly. Tie
securely at regular intervals with
string to retain its shape. Place meat,
seam side down, in deep baking dish.
2 Roast meat 1 hour 45 minutes or
until cooked. Test with a skewer; the
juices should run clear. Remove from
oven. Leave in warm place 10 minutes,
covered with foil. Remove the string
before slicing. Serve with Cider Sauce.
3 **To make Cider Sauce:** Combine

cider and stock in medium pan, bring
to boil, reduce heat to a simmer, cook,
uncovered, 15 minutes or until reduced
to 1 cup. Remove from heat, cool. Heat
butter in medium pan, add onion and
garlic, stir until soft. Add flour, stir
over low heat 2 minutes or until flour
mixture is lightly golden. Combine
reserved cider mixture with mustard
and Worcestershire sauce, add
gradually to pan, stirring until mixture
is smooth. Stir constantly over
medium heat 2 minutes or until sauce
boils and thickens, boil for a further
1 minute; remove from heat.

COOK'S FILE

Storage time: Cook this dish just
before serving. Sauce can be made a
day ahead and refrigerated.
Hint: To make crackling, cut pork rind
into small pieces. Rub generously with
lemon juice or oil, add a little salt, cook
until crisp, under a medium-hot grill.
To microwave crackling: Place rind
between paper towels; then place on a
plate and microwave on High (100 per
cent power) for about 8 minutes, or
until rind is crisp. Change the paper
once during cooking.

ROAST LEG OF PORK

Preparation time: 30 minutes
Cooking time: 3 hours 10 minutes
Serves 6 to 8

1 x 4 kg leg of pork
cooking salt

Apple Sauce
500 g green or cooking apples,
  peeled, cored and quartered
½ cup water
1 tablespoon caster sugar
60 g butter, cubed

Gravy
1 tablespoon brandy or Calvados
2 tablespoons plain flour
2 cups chicken stock

➤ PREHEAT OVEN to very hot 260°C.

1 Score pork rind with a sharp knife at 2 cm intervals. Rub in salt to ensure crisp crackling.
Place pork, rind side uppermost, on a roasting rack in a large baking dish. Add a little water to the dish. Cook for 30 minutes, or until skin begins to crackle and bubble. Reduce heat to moderate 180°C and roast for 2 hours 40 minutes (20 minutes per 500 g).

2 Baste meat occasionally with pan juices; do not cover or the crackling will soften. Remove from oven. Leave in a warm place for 10 minutes, covered with foil, before slicing. Serve with Apple Sauce and Gravy.

3 To make Apple Sauce: Place apple and water in a small pan. Cover and simmer for 10 minutes until apple is very soft. Remove from heat, stir in the sugar and butter while still warm. Sauce can be pushed through a sieve if a smoother texture is desired.

To make the Gravy: Reserve about 2 tablespoons meat juices in pan. Heat on top of stove; add brandy and stir quickly to lift sediment from bottom of pan. Cook for 1 minute. Remove from heat and stir in flour; mix well. Return pan to heat and cook for 2 minutes, stirring mixture constantly. Gradually add stock; cook, stirring occasionally, until the gravy boils and thickens. Season to taste.

C O O K ' S   F I L E

Storage time: Cook this dish just before serving. Leftover meat can be stored, covered in the refrigerator, for up to 2 days. Make sauce 1 day ahead.

1

2

3

ORANGE-GLAZED HAM

Preparation time: 10 minutes
Cooking time: 3 hours 45 minutes
Serves 20

1 x 7 kg leg ham
1 large orange
2 cups water
6 whole cloves
1¼ cups soft brown sugar
1 tablespoon mustard powder
1 cup golden syrup
1 teaspoon yellow mustard
  seeds
whole cloves

Mustard Cream
2 tablespoons French mustard
½ cup sour cream
½ cup cream

➤ PREHEAT OVEN to moderate 180°C.

1 Remove rind from ham by running a thumb around the edge, under the rind. Begin pulling from the widest edge. When rind has been removed to within 10 cm of the shank end, cut through the rind around the shank. Using a sharp knife, remove excess fat from ham; discard. Squeeze juice from orange and reserve. Peel orange rind into long, thin strips.

2 Place ham on a roasting rack in deep baking dish; add water, rind and cloves to dish. Cover ham and dish securely with foil; cook for 2 hours.

3 Remove from oven. Drain meat and reserve 1 cup of pan juices. Using a sharp knife, score the fat with deep cuts crossways and then diagonally to form a diamond pattern.

4 Combine the sugar, mustard and golden syrup in a medium bowl; mix to a thick paste. Spread half the paste thickly over the ham. Return to a

moderately hot oven 210°C, and cook, uncovered, for 30 minutes.

5 Combine reserved juice and mustard seeds with remaining brown sugar paste to make a glaze; stir until smooth.

Remove ham from oven; brush with a little glaze. Press a clove into each diamond, return to oven. Roast, uncovered, for a further hour; brushing with the glaze every 10 minutes.

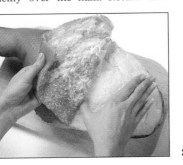

6 Place the reserved pan juices and any remaining orange and brown sugar glaze in a small pan. Stir over low heat until mixture boils; boil, without stirring, for 3 minutes. Serve ham sliced, warm or cold with brown sugar glaze and Mustard Cream.

To make Mustard Cream: Combine mustard, sour cream and cream. Leave, covered, 1 hour.

C O O K ' S   F I L E

Storage time: Cover ham with a damp cloth; store in refrigerator for about 10 days. Change cloth regularly.

4

5

6

BARBECUES & GRILLS

BARBECUED PEPPERED STEAKS WITH MANGO AND AVOCADO SALSA

Preparation time: 10 minutes
+ 30 minutes standing
Cooking time: 6 to 16 minutes
Serves 6

6 fillet steaks, about 125 g each
1-2 tablespoons whole black
    peppercorns
1 tablespoon white mustard
    seeds
2 tablespoons oil

Mango and Avocado Salsa
1 large ripe mango
1 large ripe avocado
1 spring onion, finely sliced
1 tablespoon lime juice
dash Tabasco sauce

➤ TRIM MEAT of excess fat and sinew.

1 Flatten steaks to an even thickness. Nick edges to prevent curling. Crush peppercorns and mustard seeds briefly in a blender until coarsely cracked; or, place in a paper bag and crush with a rolling pin. Spread on a plate.

2 Rub oil over the steaks, then press on the peppercorn mixture to coat. Store in refrigerator, covered with plastic wrap, for 30 minutes.

3 Place meat on a lightly oiled grill or flat plate. Cook over a high heat for 2 minutes each side to seal, turning once. For a rare result, cook a further minute each side. For medium and well done results, move meat to a cooler part of the barbecue, cook a further 2 to 3 minutes each side for medium and 4 to 6 minutes each side for well done. Serve with Mango and Avocado Salsa.

To make the Mango and Avocado Salsa: Peel mango and cut off cheeks from both sides; cut flesh into cubes. Peel avocado and cut into cubes. Combine mango, avocado and remaining ingredients in a small bowl, toss well. Refrigerate, covered, until needed.

COOK'S FILE

Storage time: Cook meat just before serving. The salsa can be prepared an hour ahead and refrigerated.

Variation: A salsa of cubed green tomatoes, chopped red onion and seeded, chopped fresh green chillies is a good accompaniment. Add salt, moisten with olive oil and vinegar.

GRILLED TERIYAKI BEEF KEBABS

Preparation time: 15 minutes
+ 2 hours marinating
Cooking time: 6 to 16 minutes
Serves 6

6 topside steaks, about
350 g each
1 cup beef stock
¼ cup teriyaki sauce
2 tablespoons hoisin sauce
2 tablespoons lime juice
1 tablespoon honey
2 spring onions, finely chopped
2 cloves garlic, crushed
1 teaspoon finely grated ginger

➤ TRIM MEAT of excess fat and sinew.

1 Slice meat across the grain evenly into long, thin strips. Thread meat on skewers, 'weaving' them in place.

2 Combine stock, sauces, lime juice, honey, spring onion, garlic and ginger in a small bowl, whisk for 1 minute or until well combined. Place skewered meat in a shallow dish, pour marinade over. Store in refrigerator, covered with plastic wrap, for 2 hours or overnight, turning occasionally. Drain, reserving marinade.

3 Place skewered meat on a cold, lightly oiled grill tray. Cook under high heat for 2 minutes each side to seal, turning once. For a rare result, cook a further 1 minute each side. For medium and well done results, lower the grill tray or reduce heat, and cook a further 2 to 3 minutes each side for medium and 4 to 6 minutes each side for well done. Brush occasionally with the reserved marinade during cooking.

COOK'S FILE

Storage time: Cook the kebabs just before serving.

Hint: For wooden skewers, soak in water 30 minutes to prevent burning.

1

2

3

OPEN-FACED FOCACCIA AND PIQUANT STEAK

Preparation time: 5 minutes
+ 30 minutes standing
Cooking time: 15 minutes
Serves 4

500 g rump steak
¼ teaspoon ground black
  pepper
1 small red onion
1 tablespoon balsamic vinegar
1 tablespoon chopped fresh
  parsley
1 large red capsicum
2 pieces focaccia, about
  12 x 10 cm
butter for spreading
10 lettuce leaves
4 anchovies, chopped
1 tablespoon capers, chopped
3 tablespoons mayonnaise
1 tablespoon Dijon mustard

➤ TRIM MEAT of excess fat and sinew; sprinkle with pepper.

1 Place meat on cold, lightly oiled grill tray. Cook meat under high heat for 3 minutes on each side or until tender. Cool to room temperature, then slice across the grain evenly into long, thin strips.

2 Slice the onion very thinly, mix with the vinegar and parsley. Leave for 30 minutes. Halve the capsicum lengthways, remove pith and seeds. Place skin side up on a cold, lightly oiled grill tray, cook under high heat for 5 minutes or until skin lifts off and blackens slightly; cool. Remove skin, slice capsicum thinly.

3 Split focaccia in half, grill on both sides until brown and crisp, spread with butter.

To assemble, place lettuce on focaccia, top with capsicum, meat, anchovies, capers and drained onion and parsley mixture. Finish off with a dollop of the combined mayonnaise and mustard.

COOK'S FILE

Storage time: Cook and assemble just before serving.

Variation: This recipe is perfect for lunch. Use other ingredients of your choice, such as sliced, ripe tomato, avocado or thin-skinned cucumber. If focaccia is unavailable, any toasted bread is suitable. Use drained, sliced, canned pimento in place of capsicum.

BEEF SATAY WITH SPICY PEANUT SAUCE

Preparation time: 20 minutes
  + 2 hours marinating
Cooking time: 10 minutes
Serves 4

1 kg blade steak
2 cloves garlic, crushed
1 tablespoon grated ginger
⅓ cup soy sauce
1 teaspoon soft brown sugar
2 tablespoons oil

Peanut Sauce
1 cup/160 g roasted peanuts
2 medium red onions, chopped
2 small red chillies, chopped
2 cloves garlic, chopped
1 teaspoon soft brown sugar
2 teaspoons grated lemon rind
1 tablespoon lemon juice
1 teaspoon ground cinnamon
1 teaspoon ground coriander
1 teaspoon turmeric
1 teaspoon ground cumin
1 tablespoon oil
1 cup coconut milk

➤ TRIM MEAT of excess fat and sinew.

1 Cut meat evenly into 3 cm cubes. Combine garlic, ginger, soy sauce, sugar and oil; add meat, stirring to coat. Store in refrigerator, covered in plastic wrap, for 2 hours or overnight, turning occasionally. Drain meat, reserving marinade.

2 Thread the meat on oiled skewers. Place satays on cold, lightly oiled grill tray. Cook under high heat 6 minutes or until tender, brushing with reserved marinade several times during cooking. Serve with Spicy Peanut Sauce.

3 **To make Spicy Peanut Sauce:** Place peanuts in a food processor bowl or blender, process until finely ground, remove. Combine onion, chilli, garlic, sugar, lemon rind, lemon juice, cinnamon, coriander, turmeric and cumin in food processor bowl or blender, process until ingredients are combined and mixture is almost smooth.

Heat oil in a medium pan, add the spice mixture, stir over medium heat for 2 minutes. Add ground peanuts, stir 1 minute. Add the coconut milk, bring to boil. Reduce heat to low, stir over heat until the sauce has reduced and thickened.

COOK'S FILE

Storage time: Cook satays just before serving. Spicy Peanut Sauce can be stored in the refrigerator, covered with plastic wrap, for up to 3 days.

1

2

3

BARBECUED CHILLI BEEF BURGERS

Preparation time: 25 minutes
+ 2 hours marinating
Cooking time: 8 minutes
Makes 18

1 kg minced beef
3 medium onions, grated
¼ cup finely chopped parsley
1½ cups/135 g packaged
    breadcrumbs
1 egg, lightly beaten
1 tablespoon milk
1 tablespoon malt vinegar
1 tablespoon tomato paste
2 tablespoons soy sauce
1 tablespoon chilli sauce
3 teaspoons dried oregano
    leaves

Mustard Butter
125 g butter, softened
2 tablespoons sour cream
2 tablespoons German mustard

➤ PLACE MINCED BEEF in a large bowl.

1 Add onion, parsley, breadcrumbs, egg, milk, vinegar, tomato paste, sauces and oregano leaves; mix well. Store in refrigerator, covered with plastic wrap, for 2 hours.

2 Divide the mixture into 18 even-sized portions; shape each portion into a burger about 1.5 cm thick.

3 Place burgers on a lightly oiled grill or a flat plate. Cook over high heat for 4 minutes each side or until well browned and cooked through. Serve the burgers with salad and dollops of Mustard Butter.

To make Mustard Butter: Beat the butter, sour cream and mustard in a small bowl for 2 minutes or until well combined. Leave the mixture, un-covered, for 20 minutes to allow the flavours to blend.

COOK'S FILE

Storage time: Cook the burgers just before serving.

1

2

3

BARBECUED MUSTARD-COATED RIB STEAKS

Preparation time: 5 minutes
  + 2 hours marinating
Cooking time: 10 to 16 minutes
Serves 6

6 rib eye steaks, about 200 g
  each, or 6 T-bone steaks
1/3 cup seeded mustard
2 tablespoons bottled salad
  dressing
1 tablespoon lemon juice
1 tablespoon chopped fresh chives
1 tablespoon honey
1 clove garlic, crushed
dash Tabasco sauce

Herbed Cream
2/3 cup sour cream
1 tablespoon finely chopped
  fresh chives
2 tablespoons finely chopped
  bottled pimento

➤ TRIM MEAT of excess fat and sinew. Flatten steaks to an even thickness. Nick edges to prevent curling.
1 Combine the mustard, salad dressing, lemon juice, chives, honey, garlic and Tabasco in a small bowl, whisk for 1 minute or until well combined. Place meat in a shallow dish, pour marinade over. Store in refrigerator, covered with plastic wrap, 2 hours or overnight, turning occasionally.
2 Place meat on lightly oiled grill or flat plate. Cook over a high heat for 2 minutes each side to seal, turning once. For a rare result, cook a further 2 to 3 minutes each side. For medium and well done results, move meat to a cooler part of the barbecue, cook a further 2 to 3 minutes each side for medium and 4 to 6 minutes each side for well done. Serve steaks with the Herbed Cream.
3 To make Herbed Cream: Mix all ingredients until well combined; the mixture should be fairly thick.

COOK'S FILE

Storage time: Cook meat just before serving. The Herbed Cream can be prepared 4 hours in advance and stored, covered, in the refrigerator.
Variation: Use fresh herbs of your choice in the Herbed Cream.

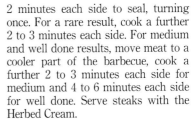

SPICY BEEF AND MINT BARBECUED SAUSAGES

Preparation time: 15 minutes
Cooking time: 10 minutes
Makes 12 sausages

750 g minced beef
250 g sausage mince
2 tablespoons cornflour
1 egg, lightly beaten
1 medium onion, finely chopped
2 cloves garlic, crushed

2 tablespoons chopped fresh
  mint
1 teaspoon sambal oelek
1 teaspoon ground cumin
1 teaspoon garam masala
1/2 teaspoon ground cardamom
1/2 cup mango chutney

➤ COMBINE MINCED BEEF and sausage mince in a bowl.
1 Add cornflour, egg, onion, garlic, mint, sambal oelek, cumin, garam masala and cardamom, mix well.
2 Divide mixture into 12 even-sized portions. Using wet hands, mould each portion into sausage shapes.
3 Place sausages on lightly oiled grill or flat plate. Cook over medium heat for 10 minutes or until cooked through; turn sausages occasionally during cooking. Serve with chutney.

COOK'S FILE

Storage time: Cook sausages just before serving.
Variation: Omit sambal oelek for a less spicy sausage. Serve the sausages with tomato sauce in place of chutney.

Barbecued Mustard-coated Rib Steaks (top), Spicy Beef and Mint Barbecued Sausages (bottom).

TERIYAKI STEAKS WITH BLUE CHEESE AND HERB BUTTER

Preparation time: 20 minutes
+ 2 hours marinating
Cooking time: 6 to 16 minutes
Serves 8

8 rib eye steaks, about
    200 g each, or 8 boneless
    sirloin steaks
¼ cup teriyaki sauce
2 cloves garlic, crushed

Blue Cheese and Herb Butter
125 g blue vein cheese, chopped
125 g butter, softened
1 tablespoon dry white wine
1 teaspoon finely chopped fresh
    mint
½ teaspoon dried rosemary
    leaves
½ teaspoon dried oregano
    leaves

➤ TRIM MEAT of excess fat and sinew.

1 Combine steaks with teriyaki sauce and garlic. Store in refrigerator, covered with plastic wrap, 2 hours or overnight, turning occasionally. Drain meat, reserving marinade.

2 Place steaks on a lightly oiled grill or flat plate. Cook over a high heat for 2 minutes each side to seal, turning once. For a rare result, cook a further minute each side. For medium and well done results, move meat to a cooler part of the barbecue, cook a further 2 to 3 minutes each side for medium and 4 to 6 minutes for well done; brush with remaining marinade in the last minutes of cooking.

Serve steaks topped with slices of Blue Cheese and Herb Butter.

3 To make Blue Cheese and

Herb Butter: Using electric beaters, beat cheese and butter in small mixing bowl until light and creamy. Add wine and herbs; beat until just combined. Spoon mixture onto a large sheet of foil. Wrap, roll and shape mixture into a log 4 x 16 cm, using a ruler as a guide. Refrigerate 4 hours or overnight.

COOK'S FILE

Storage time: Cook meat just before serving.

Hint: Herb butters are a very versatile accompaniment for barbecued meat. Use ground spices in place of herbs to add a little 'heat' to the meal.

1

2

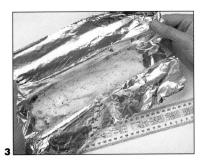

3

STEAK WITH SPEEDY BARBECUE MARINADE

Preparation time: 5 minutes
  + 2 hours marinating
Cooking time: 6 to 16 minutes
Serves 4

1 kg rump steak
1 cup red wine
2 tablespoons olive oil
1 tablespoon balsamic vinegar
1 tablespoon tomato paste
1 tablespoon Dijon mustard
1 clove garlic, crushed
2 teaspoons soft brown sugar

➤ TRIM MEAT of excess fat and sinew.

1 Combine wine, oil, vinegar, tomato paste, mustard, garlic and sugar in a small bowl, whisk for 1 minute or until well combined. Place the meat in a large dish; pour marinade over. Store in the refrigerator, covered with plastic wrap, for 2 hours or overnight, turning occasionally. Drain the meat, reserving the marinade.

2 Place meat on a lightly oiled grill or flat plate. Cook over a high heat for 2 minutes on each side, turning once. For a rare result, cook a further minute on each side. For medium and well done results, move the meat to a cooler part of the barbecue and cook for a further 2 to 3 minutes on each side for medium and 4 to 6 minutes on each side for well done; brush meat with the reserved marinade several times during cooking.

3 Leave the meat in a warm place, covered with foil, for 2 to 3 minutes. Cut it across the grain into 2 cm-thick slices for serving.

COOK'S FILE

Storage time: Cook meat just before serving.

Hint: Balsamic vinegar has a mellow flavour compared to other vinegars. It is aged in casks for at least 10 years.

1

2

3

GRILLED STEAK WITH VEGETABLE RELISH

Preparation time: 15 minutes
+ 2 hours marinating
Cooking time: 6 to 16 minutes
Serves 6

6 sirloin steaks, about
200 g each
2 tablespoons lemon juice
1 teaspoon dried thyme leaves

Vegetable Relish
2 tablespoons olive oil
1 medium onion, sliced
1 medium red capsicum, sliced
1/2 teaspoon yellow mustard
seeds
1 thin-skinned cucumber, sliced
1 large tomato, peeled, chopped
2 tablespoons malt vinegar
1 tablespoon sultanas
2 teaspoons soft brown sugar

➤ TRIM MEAT of excess fat and
sinew.
1 Combine steaks with juice and
thyme. Store in refrigerator, covered
with plastic wrap, for 2 hours or overnight, turning occasionally.
2 Place meat on a cold, lightly oiled
grill tray. Cook under a high heat for
2 minutes each side to seal, turning
once. For a rare result, cook a further
minute each side. For medium and
well done results, lower the grill tray
or reduce heat and cook a further 2 to
3 minutes each side for medium and
for 4 to 6 minutes each side for well
done. Serve with Vegetable Relish.
3 To make Vegetable Relish:
Heat oil in a small pan. Add onion, stir
over high heat 2 minutes or until well
browned and soft. Add capsicum and
mustard seeds to pan, stir over a
medium heat for 2 minutes. Add the
cucumber, tomato, vinegar, sultanas
and sugar. Bring to the boil, reduce
heat to a simmer. Cook 15 minutes,
uncovered, stirring occasionally. Serve
warm or cold.

COOK'S FILE

Storage time: Cook meat just before
serving. Vegetable Relish can be made
a day ahead and refrigerated.

1

2

3

BARBECUED FILLET STEAKS WITH LEMON MUSTARD BUTTER

Preparation time: 5 minutes
Cooking time: 6 to 16 minutes
Serves 6

6 fillet steaks, about 150 g each
1 tablespoon olive oil
2 cloves garlic, crushed
1 teaspoon ground rosemary

Lemon Mustard Butter
125 g butter
1 tablespoon French mustard
1 tablespoon lemon juice
2 teaspoons finely grated lemon rind
1 tablespoon finely chopped fresh chives

➤ TRIM MEAT of excess fat and sinew.

1 Flatten steaks to an even thickness. Nick edges to prevent curling. Combine oil, garlic and rosemary. Rub evenly over each steak.

2 Place meat on lightly oiled grill or flat plate. Cook over a high heat for 2 minutes each side to seal, turning once. For a rare result cook a further minute each side. For medium and well done results, move meat to a cooler part of the barbecue, cook for a further 2 to 3 minutes each side for medium and 4 to 6 minutes each side for well done. Serve steaks topped with a slice of Lemon Mustard Butter.

3 To make the Lemon Mustard Butter: Cream butter with mustard, lemon juice and rind. Stir in chives. Shape into a log, wrap in plastic wrap and refrigerate until required.

COOK'S FILE

Storage time: Cook meat just before serving. Lemon Mustard Butter can be prepared a day ahead and refrigerated.
Variation: A little sesame or walnut oil added to the mixture rubbed on the steaks will give them a pleasant, slightly nutty taste.

BEER-MARINATED MID-LOIN CHOPS

Preparation time: 10 minutes
+ 2 hours marinating
Cooking time: 6 to 16 minutes
Serves 6

6 mid-loin lamb chops, about
    100 g each
1 cup beer
¼ cup barbecue sauce
2 tablespoons olive oil
1 tablespoon seeded mustard
2 cloves garlic, crushed
1 small onion, finely chopped
¼ teaspoon ground black pepper

➤ TRIM MEAT of excess fat and sinew.
1 Combine beer, barbecue sauce, oil, mustard, garlic, onion and pepper in a small bowl, whisk for 1 minute or until well combined. Place chops in shallow dish, pour over marinade.
2 Store in refrigerator, covered with plastic wrap, for 2 hours or overnight, turning occasionally. Drain and reserve marinade.
3 Place meat on a lightly oiled grill or flat plate. Cook over a high heat for 2 minutes each side to seal, turning once. For a rare result, cook a further minute each side. For medium and well done results, move meat to a cooler part of the barbecue and cook a further 2 to 3 minutes each side for medium and 4 to 6 minutes each side for well done; brush the chops with the reserved marinade several times during cooking.

COOK'S FILE

Storage time: Cook meat just before serving.
Variation: Alcohol in a marinade flavours and tenderises the meat. Use a full-bodied beer such as Guinness to get the best result. Substitute red wine for beer, if preferred. Choose a strong mustard for an additional impact. Marinate meat overnight, if possible. The longer the marinating, the better the flavour of the cooked item.

GREEK LAMB KEBABS

Preparation time: 20 minutes
+ 2 hours marinating
Cooking time: 12 minutes
Makes 20 kebabs

1.5 kg boned leg of lamb
⅓ cup olive oil
¼ cup lemon juice
2 tablespoons dry white wine
2 cloves garlic, crushed
2 tablespoons soy sauce
1 teaspoon dried oregano
    leaves
½ teaspoon ground black
    pepper
1 large onion, finely chopped
¼ cup finely chopped fresh
    parsley

➤ TRIM MEAT of excess fat and sinew. Cut the meat evenly into 3 cm cubes.
1 Thread cubed meat onto oiled skewers. Place oil, juice, wine, garlic, sauce, oregano and pepper in a small bowl. Whisk together for 2 minutes or until well combined. Pour over meat.
2 Store, covered with plastic wrap, in the refrigerator for 2 hours or overnight, turning occasionally. Drain meat, reserving the marinade.
3 Place meat on a cold, lightly oiled grill tray. Cook under a high heat for 12 minutes or until tender, turning once. Brush with reserved marinade several times during cooking. Combine onion and parsley; serve sprinkled over the kebabs.

COOK'S FILE

Storage time: Cook the kebabs just before serving.
Variation: Worcestershire sauce or an Asian condiment such as hoisin sauce can be used in place of soy.

Beer-marinated Mid-loin Chops (top),
Greek Lamb Kebabs (bottom).

BARBECUED SPICY LAMB KOFTAS

Preparation time: 10 minutes
  + 1 hour standing
Cooking time: 10 minutes
Serves 6

500 g minced lamb
1 medium onion, finely chopped
1 clove garlic, crushed
2 tablespoons chopped fresh
  mint
1 teaspoon ground coriander
1 teaspoon ground cardamom
¼ teaspoon curry powder
pinch cayenne pepper

½ cup/about 45 g packaged
  breadcrumbs
1 egg, lightly beaten
1 cup/about 90 g packaged
  breadcrumbs, extra

Yoghurt Dressing
⅔ cup plain yoghurt
1 tablespoon chopped fresh
  coriander
2 teaspoons chopped fresh mint
½ teaspoon grated lemon rind

➤ PLACE MINCED LAMB in a medium bowl.

1 Add onion, garlic, herbs, spices and breadcrumbs. Mix together well using your hands. Divide meat mixture into 12 even portions. Mould into sausage shapes around oiled, metal skewers.

2 Brush lightly with egg; roll in extra breadcrumbs to coat evenly. Store in the refrigerator, covered with plastic wrap, 1 hour or overnight.

3 Place skewers on a lightly greased grill or flat plate. Cook over medium heat for 10 minutes or until cooked through, turning occasionally. Serve with Yoghurt Dressing.

To make Yoghurt Dressing: Beat all the ingredients in a small bowl until well combined. Refrigerate.

COOK'S FILE

Storage time: Cook the koftas just before serving.

SPICED LAMB WITH CUCUMBER SALSA

Preparation time: 15 minutes
+ 2 hours marinating
Cooking time: 30 to 40 minutes
Serves 6

1 x 1.5 kg leg of lamb,
   boned
2/3 cup plain yoghurt
1 medium onion, chopped
1 teaspoon grated ginger
1 teaspoon ground cumin
1 teaspoon ground coriander
1 teaspoon poppy seeds
1 teaspoon turmeric
1/2 teaspoon garam masala
1/4 teaspoon ground nutmeg

Cucumber Salsa
1 thin-skinned cucumber, cut
   into 1 cm cubes
1 small tomato, cut into
   1 cm cubes
1 small red onion, thinly sliced
grated rind and juice of 1 lime
1 tablespoon chopped fresh
   coriander
1 tablespoon chopped fresh basil
1 teaspoon soft brown sugar

➤ TRIM MEAT of excess fat and
sinew. Flatten out the leg.
1 Combine yoghurt, onion, ginger,
cumin, coriander, poppy seeds,
turmeric, garam masala and nutmeg in
food processor bowl or blender,
process 10 seconds or until smooth.
2 Place meat in a large dish. Spread
yoghurt mixture over meat, turn lamb
until well coated. Store in refrigerator,
covered with plastic wrap, for 2 hours
or overnight. Bring to room temperature before cooking.
3 Place meat on cold, lightly oiled
grill tray. Cook under medium heat for

30 minutes, turning once. Cook a further 5 minutes for a medium result and
10 minutes for well done. Serve sliced
with Cucumber Salsa.
4 To make Cucumber Salsa: Combine ingredients in a bowl; mix well.

COOK'S FILE

Storage time: Cook meat just before
serving.
Hint: To avoid meat burning, cook on
lowest level of grill compartment.

BARBECUED PORK SPARERIBS

Preparation time: 5 minutes
  + 2 hours marinating
Cooking time: 20 minutes
Serves 6 to 8

1 kg pork spareribs
2 tablespoons tomato paste
2 tablespoons hoisin sauce
2 tablespoons chilli sauce
1/4 cup lemon juice
1/4 cup honey
2 tablespoons sesame seeds,
  toasted

➤ REMOVE RIND from spareribs. Trim excess fat.

1 Combine tomato paste, hoisin and chilli sauces, lemon juice and honey. Place ribs in a large, shallow dish. Pour marinade over.
Store in refrigerator, covered with plastic wrap, for 2 hours or overnight, turning occasionally. Drain meat, reserving the marinade.

2 Place the ribs on lightly oiled grill or flat plate. Cook over a medium heat for 20 minutes or until tender, turning occasionally.

3 Heat the remaining marinade in a small pan over low heat; do not boil. Pour over the ribs just before serving.

Sprinkle with the toasted sesame seeds.

COOK'S FILE

Storage time: Cook spareribs just before serving.

Variation: Marinades are quick and easy to make and turn a basically simple recipe into something special. For an alternative marinade, combine 1/3 cup soy sauce, 2 tablespoons dry sherry, 1 tablespoon black bean sauce, 1 teaspoon five spice powder, 1 clove garlic, crushed and 1/4 teaspoon ground black pepper. Sprinkle with roasted, unsalted, crushed cashew nuts or peanuts.

BARBECUED SKEWERED LAMB

Preparation time: 10 minutes
  + 2 hours marinating
Cooking time: 8 minutes
Serves 8

500 g lamb, cut into cubes
2 medium red onions, cut into
  eighths
200 g punnet cherry tomatoes

Lemon Marinade
2 tablespoons lemon juice

2 teaspoons grated lemon rind
1/4 cup olive oil
1/4 cup dry white wine
2 cloves garlic, crushed
1/2 teaspoon dried oregano
  leaves
1/2 teaspoon ground cumin
1/4 teaspoon ground cinnamon

➤ TRIM MEAT of excess fat and sinew.

1 To make the Lemon Marinade: Whisk all ingredients in a small bowl for 2 minutes or until well combined. Place meat in a shallow dish, pour marinade over, stirring well to coat.

Store in refrigerator, covered with plastic wrap, for 2 hours or overnight, turning occasionally. Drain meat, reserving marinade.

2 Thread meat, onion wedges and tomatoes alternately onto oiled skewers. Place kebabs on a lightly oiled grill or flat plate.

3 Cook over medium-high heat for 8 minutes or until tender, brushing with reserved marinade several times during cooking.

COOK'S FILE

Storage time: Cook this dish just before serving.

Barbecued Pork Spareribs (top),
Barbecued Skewered Lamb (bottom).

BARBECUED PORK MEDALLIONS WITH OLIVE TAPENADE

Preparation time: 20 minutes
Cooking time: 10 minutes
Serves 4

4 x 200 g pork butterfly
  medallions or 4 pork loin
  medallion steaks, about
  150 g each
2 tablespoons olive oil
1 tablespoon lemon juice
1 tablespoon fresh thyme leaves
¼ teaspoon ground black
  pepper

Olive Tapenade
2 tablespoons olive oil
½ small onion, finely chopped
1 clove garlic, crushed
125 g pitted black olives, finely
  chopped
2 anchovies, finely chopped
1 small, ripe tomato, peeled,
  seeded and chopped
2 teaspoons balsamic vinegar
1 medium red chilli, finely
  chopped
1 tablespoon chopped fresh
  basil leaves

➤ IF USING pork loin medallion steaks, shape into rounds by securing thinner tail end to the medallion with toothpicks.

1 Trim meat of excess fat and sinew.

2 Combine oil, lemon juice, thyme and pepper, brush over meat.

3 Place meat on lightly oiled flat plate or grill. Cook over medium heat for 5 minutes on each side or until tender. Serve with Tapenade.

4 To make Olive Tapenade: Heat the oil in small pan, add onion and garlic, stir until onion is tender. Add olives, anchovies, tomato, vinegar, chilli and basil, stir 1 minute to combine. Serve hot or cold.

COOK'S FILE

Storage time: Cook meat just before serving. Tapenade can be made and stored in an airtight container in the refrigerator for up to 3 days.

Hint: Tapenade is a salty, strongly flavoured accompaniment, ideal with meats such as pork which have a mild, subtle flavour. Other more traditional, full-flavoured accompaniments are stewed prunes or apples and braised sauerkraut.

Unless it is cooked carefully over a moderate heat, pork can become dry; because it is a close-textured meat, it also can become tough. Cuts such as those used in this recipe are done when the flesh feels fairly firm to the touch; it should still be juicy and a very faint pink.

1

2

3

4

STIR-FRIES

BEEF WITH BLACK BEAN SAUCE

Preparation time: 15 minutes
+ 1 hour marinating
Cooking time: 10 minutes
Serves 4

750 g rump steak
2 cloves garlic, crushed
2 teaspoons grated ginger
2 tablespoons dry sherry
1 tablespoon soy sauce
2 teaspoons cornflour
3 tablespoons peanut oil
2 medium onions, cut into
   wedges
1 large green capsicum, cut into
   strips
1 x 230 g can sliced bamboo
   shoots, drained
2 tablespoons canned black
   beans, rinsed, chopped
1 teaspoon cornflour, extra
1 tablespoon chicken stock

➤ TRIM MEAT of any fat and sinew.
1 Slice meat across the grain evenly into long, thin strips. Combine the garlic, ginger, sherry, soy sauce and cornflour; add meat, stirring to coat. Store in refrigerator, covered with plastic wrap, 1 hour or overnight, turning occasionally. Drain meat. Reserve marinade.
2 Heat 2 tablespoons of the oil in wok or heavy-based frying pan, swirling gently to coat base and side. Cook the meat quickly in small batches over high heat until browned but not cooked through. Remove from wok; drain on absorbent paper.
Heat remaining oil in wok, swirling gently to coat base and side. Add onion and capsicum, stir-fry over high heat for 3 minutes or until onion is soft. Add bamboo shoots and black beans, stir-fry over high heat 1 minute.
3 Combine the extra cornflour and remaining marinade with stock until smooth, add to wok with meat, stir-fry over high heat until meat is cooked through and sauce has thickened. Remove from heat, serve immediately. Serve with rice.

COOK'S FILE

Storage time: Cook this dish just before serving.
Hint: Store the leftover black beans in an airtight jar in the refrigerator for up to 2 weeks.

1

2

3

BEEF AND ASPARAGUS

Preparation time: 15 minutes
+ 30 minutes marinating
Cooking time: 10 minutes
Serves 4

500 g rump steak
2 tablespoons soy sauce
1 tablespoon dry sherry
2 teaspoons finely
    grated ginger
1 teaspoon sesame oil
1 clove garlic, crushed
1 medium red chilli, cut into
    fine strips
12 spears fresh asparagus
2 tablespoons peanut oil
1 teaspoon cornflour

➤ TRIM MEAT of any fat and
sinew.
1 Slice meat across the grain evenly
into long, thin strips. Combine soy
sauce, sherry, ginger, sesame oil, garlic
and chilli; add meat, stirring to coat.
Leave 30 minutes. Drain the meat,
reserving marinade.
2 Cut woody ends off asparagus; cut
spears into 5 cm pieces. Heat 1 tablespoon oil in a wok or heavy-based
frying pan, swirling gently to coat
base and side. Add asparagus; stir-fry
over medium heat for 2 minutes.
Remove from wok. Keep warm.

Heat remaining oil in wok, swirling
gently to coat base and side; cook meat
quickly in small batches over a high
heat until browned but not cooked
through. Remove from wok; drain on
absorbent paper.
3 Blend cornflour with the reserved
marinade until smooth. Return
asparagus and meat to wok with
marinade mixture. Stir-fry over high
heat until meat is cooked and sauce
has thickened. Serve at once.

COOK'S FILE

Storage time: Cook this dish just
before serving.
Hint: Canned asparagus is not
suitable for this recipe.

1

2

3

BEEF AND SESAME PLUM STIR-FRY

Preparation time: 30 minutes
+ 1 hour marinating
Cooking time: 20 minutes
Serves 4

750 g beef fillet
½ cup bottled chunky
  tomato sauce
½ cup plum sauce
1 tablespoon soy sauce
1 teaspoon chilli sauce
2 tablespoons sesame seeds
1 tablespoon peanut oil
2 teaspoons sesame oil
1 large carrot, cut into fine
  strips
2 sticks celery, cut into fine
  strips
1 large zucchini, cut into fine
  strips
1 medium red capsicum, cut
  into fine strips
1 medium onion, cut into wedges

➤ TRIM MEAT of any fat and sinew. Cut meat into 4 even pieces lengthways.

1 Slice meat across the grain evenly into thin strips. Combine tomato, plum, soy and chilli sauces; add meat, stirring to coat. Store in refrigerator, covered with plastic wrap, for 1 hour or overnight, turning occasionally.

2 Place sesame seeds in a small pan, stir over medium heat until golden. Remove from pan.

Heat the oils in a wok or heavy-based frying pan, swirling gently to coat base and side. Add carrot, stir-fry over medium heat for 3 minutes. Add the celery, zucchini, capsicum and onion, stir-fry over medium heat 4 minutes or until vegetables are tender. Remove from wok, keep warm.

3 Reheat the wok, cook meat and marinade quickly in small batches over high heat until browned but not cooked through. Remove from wok; drain on absorbent paper. Return meat to wok, stir-fry over high heat until cooked and sauce has thickened. Serve spooned over the vegetable strips; sprinkle with the sesame seeds.

COOK'S FILE

Storage time: Cook this dish just before serving.

Hint: Finely cut vegetables cook fast.

1

2

3

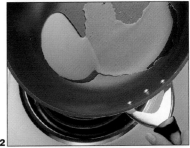

BEEF WITH CAPSICUM AND OYSTER SAUCE

Preparation time: 15 minutes
Cooking time: 8 minutes
Serves 6

500 g rump steak
1 tablespoon soy sauce
1 egg white, lightly beaten
1 tablespoon cornflour
¼ teaspoon ground black pepper
2 tablespoons peanut oil
1 tablespoon grated fresh ginger
¼ teaspoon Chinese five spice powder
1 small green capsicum, cut in diamond shapes
1 small red capsicum, cut in diamond shapes
2 sticks celery, thinly sliced
1 x 425 g can whole baby corn, drained
2 tablespoons oyster sauce
2 spring onions, diagonally sliced

➤ TRIM MEAT of any fat and sinew.

1 Slice meat across the grain evenly into long, thin strips. Combine the soy sauce, egg white, cornflour and pepper; add meat, stirring to coat.

2 Heat 1 tablespoon oil in a wok or heavy-based pan, swirling gently to coat base and side. Add the ginger, five spice powder, capsicum, celery and corn and stir-fry over high heat for 2 minutes or until just beginning to soften; remove from wok; keep warm.

3 Heat remaining oil in wok, swirling gently to coat base and side. Cook meat quickly in small batches over a high heat until browned but not cooked through. Remove from wok; drain on absorbent paper.

4 Return meat and vegetables to wok with oyster sauce. Stir-fry over high heat until meat is cooked and sauce is hot. Remove from heat; serve immediately, sprinkled with spring onion.

COOK'S FILE

Storage time: Cook this dish just before serving.

BEEF AND WALNUT STIR-FRY

Preparation time: 20 minutes
+ 2 hours marinating
Cooking time: 15 minutes
Serves 6

1 kg rump steak
2 teaspoons grated ginger
2 cloves garlic, crushed
2 spring onions, finely
   chopped
¼ cup soy sauce
¼ cup oyster sauce
2 tablespoons dry sherry
2 tablespoons peanut oil
½ cup walnut pieces
1 large red capsicum,
   cut into thin strips
2 teaspoons sesame oil
½ teaspoon cornflour
¼ cup chicken stock

➤ TRIM MEAT of any fat and
sinew.

1 Slice meat across the grain evenly
into long, thin strips. Combine ginger,
garlic, spring onion, soy and oyster
sauces and sherry; add meat, stirring
to coat. Store in the refrigerator,
covered with plastic wrap, for 2 hours
or overnight, turning occasionally.
Drain the meat, reserving the
marinade.

2 Heat 1 tablespoon oil in a wok or
heavy-based frying pan, swirling
gently to coat base and side. Add
walnuts, stir-fry over a high heat for
1 minute or until lightly golden. Add
capsicum, stir-fry over a high heat for
2 minutes; remove from wok; keep
warm. Heat remaining oil and sesame
oil in wok, swirling gently to coat base
and side. Cook meat quickly in small
batches over a high heat until browned
but not cooked through. Remove from
wok; drain on absorbent paper.

3 Blend cornflour with reserved
marinade and stock until smooth.
Return vegetables and meat to wok
with marinade mixture. Stir-fry over
high heat until meat is cooked and
sauce has thickened. Remove from
heat, serve immediately.

COOK'S FILE

Storage time: Cook this dish just
before serving.

BEEF AND BROCCOLI STIR-FRY

Preparation time: 10 minutes
+ 2 hours marinating
Cooking time: 15 minutes
Serves 4

750 g rump steak
2 tablespoons cornflour
1 tablespoon soy sauce
1 tablespoon dry sherry
1 teaspoon grated ginger
¼ cup peanut oil
1 large carrot, cut into long, thin strips
300 g piece broccoli, cut into small florets

2 tablespoons sweet chilli sauce
½ cup beef stock

➤ TRIM MEAT of any fat and sinew.

1 Slice meat across the grain evenly into long, wide strips. Combine cornflour, soy sauce, sherry and ginger; add meat, stirring to coat. Store in refrigerator, covered with plastic wrap, 2 hours or overnight, turning occasionally. Drain meat, reserving marinade.

2 Heat 1 tablespoon of the oil in wok or heavy-based frying pan, swirling gently to coat base and side. Add the carrot and broccoli, stir-fry over high heat 4 minutes. Remove from wok; keep warm.

Heat remaining oil in wok, swirling gently to coat base and side. Cook meat quickly in small batches over high heat until browned but not cooked through. Remove from wok; drain on absorbent paper.

3 Combine sauce, stock and reserved marinade. Add to the wok, stir over medium heat until mixture boils. Return broccoli, carrrot and meat to wok. Stir-fry over medium heat until meat is cooked and the broccoli is just tender. Remove from the heat, serve immediately.

COOK'S FILE

Storage time: Cook just before serving.
Variation: Add a little chopped fresh chilli for a hotter result, if desired.

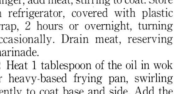

CHILLI LAMB AND CASHEWS

Preparation time: 10 minutes
Cooking time: 10 minutes
Serves 4

750 g lamb fillets
4 tablespoons peanut oil
1 cup/150 g cashews
1 large onion, cut into wedges
200 g snow peas
1 x 230 g can sliced bamboo shoots, drained

2 tablespoons chilli sauce
1 tablespoon soy sauce

➤ TRIM MEAT of any fat and sinew. Slice meat across the grain evenly into thin slices.

1 Heat 2 tablespoons of the oil in a wok or heavy-based frying pan, swirling gently to coat base and side; cook meat quickly in small batches over a high heat until browned but not cooked through. Remove from wok; drain on absorbent paper.

2 Wipe out wok with absorbent paper. Heat 1 tablespoon oil; fry the

cashews until golden brown. Remove from wok with a slotted spoon; drain on absorbent paper.

3 Heat remaining oil in wok, swirling gently to coat base and side. Add onion and snow peas; stir-fry over medium heat for 2 minutes. Add the bamboo shoots; stir-fry 1 minute. Return meat to wok with the cashews, chilli and soy sauces. Stir-fry over high heat until meat is cooked and sauce is hot. Serve immediately.

COOK'S FILE

Storage time: Cook just before serving.

Beef and Broccoli Stir-fry (top),
Chilli Lamb and Cashews (bottom).

SATAY LAMB WITH NOODLES

Preparation time: 15 minutes
Cooking time: 10 minutes
Serves 4

750 g lamb fillets
¼ cup peanut oil
3 large onions, cut in thin
 wedges
⅓ cup crunchy peanut butter
2 tablespoons hoisin sauce
½ cup coconut milk
¼ teaspoon garam masala
100 g dried egg noodles
3 teaspoons sesame oil
2 spring onions, finely chopped

➤ TRIM LAMB of any fat and sinew.

1 Slice meat across the grain evenly into thin slices. Heat 1 tablespoon of the oil in a wok or heavy-based frying pan, swirling gently to coat base and side. Add the onion, stir-fry over high heat for 5 minutes. Remove from wok; keep warm.

2 Heat remaining oil in wok, swirling gently to coat base and side. Cook meat quickly in small batches over high heat until browned but not cooked through. Remove from wok; drain on absorbent paper.

3 Combine peanut butter, hoisin sauce, coconut milk and garam masala in a small bowl. Add to wok, stir over a medium heat until mixture boils. Return the meat and onion to wok, stir until coated with sauce and just heated through.

4 Cook the noodles in a large pan of rapidly boiling water until just tender; drain. Toss with sesame oil and spring onion. Serve noodles topped with satay lamb.

COOK'S FILE

Storage time: Cook this dish just before serving.

Hint: Dried egg noodles are available in specialty Asian stores, sold in small, tangled bunches. Fresh egg noodles are also available; these need only very brief cooking in boiling water. There are many varieties of wheat and rice noodle, each varying slightly in texture and flavour. Experiment with different types for this recipe.

1

2

3

4

MONGOLIAN LAMB

Preparation time: 15 minutes
+ 1 hour marinating
Cooking time: 10 minutes
Serves 4

750 g lamb fillets
2 cloves garlic, crushed
1 teaspoon grated fresh ginger
1 tablespoon sesame oil
2 tablespoons peanut oil
4 medium onions, cut in wedges
3 teaspoons cornflour
1 tablespoon soy sauce
¼ cup dry sherry
1 tablespoon toasted sesame
  seeds (see Hint)

➤ TRIM MEAT of any fat and sinew.

1 Slice meat across the grain evenly into thin slices. Combine garlic, ginger and sesame oil; add meat, stirring to coat. Store in refrigerator, covered with plastic wrap, 1 hour or overnight, turning occasionally.

2 Heat peanut oil in wok or heavy-based frying pan, swirling gently to coat base and side. Add onion, stir-fry over medium heat for 4 minutes or until soft, remove from wok; keep warm. Reheat wok, cook the meat quickly in small batches over high heat until browned but not cooked through. Remove from wok; drain on absorbent paper.

3 Combine cornflour, soy sauce and sherry to make a smooth paste. Return meat to wok with cornflour mixture, stir-fry over high heat until meat is cooked and sauce has thickened. Remove from heat, spoon over onion, sprinkle with sesame seeds.

COOK'S FILE

Storage time: Cook this dish just before serving.

Hint: Once opened, sesame oil must be stored in an airtight container in the refrigerator; oils made from nuts tend to turn rancid in hot weather.

To toast sesame seeds, place in pan, stir over medium heat until golden.

Partially freeze meat before slicing. It is much easier to cut very thin slices from semi-frozen meat.

1

2

3

SWEET AND SOUR PORK SPARERIBS

Preparation time: 5 minutes
Cooking time: 20 minutes
Serves 6

1 kg pork spareribs
¼ cup cornflour
¼ cup peanut oil
6 spring onions, cut into
   2.5 cm slices
1 small red capsicum, cut into
   diamond shapes
1 small green capsicum, cut
   into diamond shapes
2 stalks celery, thinly sliced
¼ cup unsweetened pineapple
   juice
2 tablespoons white vinegar
2 tablespoons soy sauce
1 tablespoon tomato paste
1 tablespoon soft brown sugar
2 teaspoons cornflour, extra
½ cup chicken stock

➤ TRIM ANY rind and excess fat from spareribs.

1 Boil ribs in large pot of water. Simmer for 10 minutes; drain. Pat dry with absorbent paper.

2 Cut each sparerib in two. Dust with cornflour and shake off excess. Heat oil in a wok or heavy-based frying pan, swirling gently to coat base and side. Cook spareribs quickly in batches over high heat for about 10 minutes or until golden. Remove from wok and drain well on absorbent paper. Keep warm.

3 Add all vegetables to wok, stir-fry over high heat for 3 minutes until beginning to soften but still crisp. Remove from wok; keep warm.

4 Combine pineapple juice, vinegar, soy sauce, tomato paste and sugar in a small bowl; add to wok. Combine the cornflour and chicken stock to make a smooth paste. Stir into sauce mixture in wok and cook until liquid boils and thickens. Return the spareribs and vegetables to wok; simmer 2 minutes. Serve with steamed rice.

COOK'S FILE

Storage time: Cook this dish just before serving.

Hint: Always trim spareribs well, or buy them as lean as possible. If there is too much fat, it will spoil the taste of the dish.

Supply finger bowls and plenty of napkins when serving spareribs as they are one of the messiest of foods!

Peanut oil is the best oil for stir-frying. It has a mild flavour that does not 'compete' with the other ingredients. It can be heated safely to the required high temperature. Strain after use to remove any food particles. Use a maximum of three times; then discard.

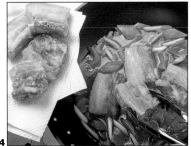

PAN-FRIES

BEEF STROGANOFF

Preparation time: 25 minutes
Cooking time: 12 minutes
Serves 6

1 kg piece rump steak
⅓ cup plain flour
¼ teaspoon ground black
  pepper
¼ cup olive oil
1 large onion, chopped
500 g baby mushrooms
1 tablespoon ground sweet paprika
1 tablespoon tomato paste
2 teaspoons French mustard
½ cup dry white wine
¼ cup chicken stock
¾ cup sour cream
1 tablespoon finely chopped
  fresh parsley

➤ TRIM MEAT of excess fat and sinew.

1 Slice meat across the grain evenly into short, thin pieces. Combine flour and pepper on a sheet of greaseproof paper. Toss meat in seasoned flour; shake off excess.

2 Heat 2 tablespoons oil in a heavy-based pan. Cook meat quickly in small batches over medium-high heat until well browned; drain on absorbent paper.

3 Add remaining oil to pan. Add the onion, cook over a medium heat for 3 minutes or until soft. Add mushrooms, stir over medium heat 5 minutes.

4 Add the paprika, tomato paste, mustard, wine and stock to pan, bring to the boil. Reduce heat and simmer for 5 minutes, uncovered, stirring occasionally. Return meat to pan with sour cream, stir until combined and just heated through. Sprinkle with parsley just before serving.

COOK'S FILE

Storage time: Cook several hours ahead, omitting the sour cream and parsley; store in refrigerator. Reheat gently, adding the final ingredients.

STEAK DIANE

Preparation time: 5 minutes
Cooking time: 6 to 16 minutes
Serves 6

6 fillet steaks, about 130 g each
½ teaspoon ground black
  pepper
45 g butter
20 g butter, extra
4 cloves garlic, crushed
2 spring onions, finely
  chopped
2 tablespoons Worcestershire
  sauce

1 tablespoon brandy
½ cup cream
2 tablespoons finely chopped
  fresh parsley

➤ TRIM MEAT of excess fat and
sinew. Flatten steaks to an even thickness. Nick edges to prevent curling.
Sprinkle each steak with pepper.

1 Heat butter in pan; add steaks.
Cook over high heat 2 minutes each
side to seal, turning once. For a rare
result, cook a further minute each side.
For medium and well done results,
reduce heat to medium, cook a further
2 to 3 minutes each side for medium
and 4 to 6 minutes each side for well

done. Remove from pan; drain on absorbent paper.

2 Heat extra butter in pan. Add garlic
and spring onion and cook gently for
3 minutes. Add Worcestershire sauce
and brandy and stir to dislodge crusty
pieces from bottom of pan.

3 Stir in the cream; simmer 5 minutes.
Return steaks to pan with parsley and
heat through.

COOK'S FILE

Storage time: Cook just before serving.
Hint: Have all the ingredients ready
before beginning; the highlight of this
dish is the tender meat cooked to just
the right degree.

PEPPER STEAKS WITH RED WINE SAUCE

Preparation time: 10 minutes
Cooking time: 8 to 18 minutes
Serves 4

4 fillet steaks, 4 cm thick,
   about 300 g each
2 tablespoons ground black
   pepper
1 tablespoon oil
15 g butter
1 medium onion, cut in wedges
2 cloves garlic, crushed
⅓ cup red wine

2 tablespoons brandy
1 cup beef stock
2 tablespoons chopped fresh
   parsley
30 g butter, extra

➤ TRIM MEAT of excess fat and sinew. Sprinkle each steak with a little pepper.

1 Heat oil and butter in pan, add steaks. Cook over high heat 3 minutes on each side to seal, turning once. For a rare result, cook a further minute on each side. For medium and well done results, reduce heat to medium, cook a further 2 to 3 minutes each side for medium and 4 to 6 minutes each side for well done. Remove from pan, keep warm.

2 Add onion and garlic to pan, cook until soft. Add wine, brandy and stock, bring to the boil. Reduce heat to a simmer, cook, uncovered, 5 minutes or until reduced by half.

3 Add parsley and extra butter, stir until combined, pour over steaks.

COOK'S FILE

Storage time: Cook this dish just before serving.

Hint: To keep steaks warm, place on an ovenproof tray and cover with foil. Leave for a short time in a very slow oven 120°C.

1

2

3

MARINATED T-BONE STEAKS

Preparation time: 5 minutes
+ 2 hours marinating
Cooking time: 6 to 16 minutes
Serves 6

6 T-bone steaks,
    about 330 g each
2 cloves garlic, crushed
1 large onion, finely chopped
½ teaspoon ground oregano
¼ teaspoon ground cumin
¼ teaspoon chilli powder
2 teaspoons soft brown sugar
2 tablespoons tomato paste
1 beef stock cube, crumbled
½ cup water
¼ cup red wine
1 tablespoon oil
1 teaspoon cornflour

➤ TRIM MEAT of excess fat and sinew. Flatten steaks to an even thickness. Nick edges to prevent curling.

1 Mix garlic, onion, oregano, cumin, chilli, sugar, tomato paste, stock cube, water and wine in a mixing bowl until well combined. Place meat in a large, shallow dish; spoon marinade over. Store in refrigerator, covered with plastic wrap, for 2 hours or overnight, turning occasionally. Drain meat, reserving marinade.

2 Heat oil in pan; add steaks. Cook over high heat 2 minutes each side to seal, turning once. For a rare result, cook a further minute each side. For medium and well done, reduce heat to medium, cook a further 2 to 3 minutes each side for medium and 4 to 6 minutes each side for well done. Remove from pan; drain on absorbent paper; keep warm.

3 Place reserved marinade in a small pan. Combine cornflour with a little cold water to make a smooth paste.

Add to marinade in pan, stir over medium heat for 5 minutes or until sauce boils and thickens; strain. Serve over steaks.

COOK'S FILE

Storage time: Cook this dish just before serving.

1

2

3

QUICK STEAK AND ONIONS WITH SATAY SAUCE

Preparation time: 5 minutes
Cooking time: 6 to 16 minutes
Serves 4

4 rib eye steaks or
  boneless sirloin steaks,
  about 150 g each
1 tablespoon oil
15 g butter
2 medium onions, cut into
  wedges
3 tablespoons bottled satay
  sauce
3 tablespoons plain yoghurt
2 teaspoons chopped fresh
  coriander
1 tablespoon chopped fresh mint

➤ TRIM MEAT of excess fat and sinew.

1 Heat oil and butter in pan, add meat. Cook over high heat 2 minutes each side to seal, turning once. For a rare result, cook a further minute on each side. For medium and well done results, reduce heat to medium, cook a further 2 to 3 minutes each side for medium and 4 to 6 minutes each side for well done. Remove steaks from pan, keep warm.

2 Add the onion to pan, cook over medium heat until soft. Place on top of meat, keep warm.

3 Add satay sauce to pan, bring to the boil. Reduce heat to a simmer, stir in yoghurt, coriander and mint. Reheat without boiling. To serve, spoon sauce over the steaks and onion wedges.

COOK'S FILE

Storage time: Cook this dish just before serving.

Variation: The sauce for this dish can be used over thin strips of stir-fried beef or pork.

Hint: Never allow yoghurt to come to the boil because it will curdle, spoiling the appearance and flavour of the finished dish.

CRUNCHY POLENTA SCHNITZEL WITH RATATOUILLE

Preparation time: 30 minutes
Cooking time: 1 hour
Serves 4

4 thin slices topside steak,
　about 150 g each
⅓ cup grated Parmesan cheese
3 tablespoons plain flour
1 egg, lightly beaten
1½ cups coarse polenta
2 tablespoons oil
30 g butter

Ratatouille
2 tablespoons oil
1 medium onion, sliced
2 cloves garlic, crushed
1 medium eggplant,
　cut into 3 cm cubes
2 medium zucchini,
　cut into 1.5 cm slices
1 medium green capsicum,
　seeded and thinly sliced
1 x 440 g can tomatoes with
　their liquid, crushed
1 cup water
1 tablespoon tomato paste
1 tablespoon chopped
　fresh basil
1 tablespoon chopped fresh
　parsley

➤ TRIM MEAT of excess fat and sinew. Flatten the steaks to an even thickness.

1 Spoon Parmesan cheese on one half of each steak, fold steak over to enclose cheese. Pound edges of steak together to seal.

2 Place flour on a sheet of grease-proof paper. Toss steaks in flour, shake off excess. Dip in egg, coat with polenta, pressing it on firmly.

3 Heat oil and butter in heavy-based pan; add meat. Cook over medium heat 2 to 3 minutes each side, turning once. Remove from the pan, drain on absorbent paper.

4 To make Ratatouille: Heat oil in pan, add onion, stir over medium heat for 2 minutes or until soft. Add garlic, eggplant, zucchini and capsicum, cook further 3 minutes. Add tomatoes, water and tomato paste, bring to the boil. Reduce heat and simmer, covered, for 45 minutes or until vegetables are tender, stirring often. Stir in basil and parsley; serve.

COOK'S FILE

Storage time: Cook meat just before serving. Ratatouille can be cooked up to 4 days ahead. Store in refrigerator, covered with plastic wrap.

Hint: If necessary, add a little extra water to the Ratatouille during cooking to prevent the mixture becoming dry and sticking to the pan. Ratatouille is delicious served either hot or cold.

RUMP STEAKS WITH MUSHROOM SAUCE

Preparation time: 10 minutes
Cooking time: 6 to 16 minutes
Serves 4

4 rump steaks, about 300 g each
¼ cup olive oil
350 g baby mushrooms, sliced
2 tablespoons sweet white wine
½ cup chicken stock
½ cup cream
1 teaspoon dried basil leaves
1 clove garlic, crushed

➤ TRIM MEAT of excess fat and sinew.

1 Heat 2 tablespoons oil in pan; add steaks. Cook over high heat 2 minutes each side to seal, turning once. For a rare result, cook a further minute each side. For medium and well done results, reduce heat to medium, cook a further 2 to 3 minutes each side for medium and 4 to 6 minutes each side for well done. Remove meat from pan; drain on absorbent paper. Keep warm.

2 Heat the remaining oil in pan. Add mushroooms, stir over medium heat for 5 minutes or until well browned. Add wine, stock, cream and basil.

3 Bring to the boil; boil, uncovered, for 2 minutes, or until sauce thickens slightly, stirring constantly. Add the garlic; remove from heat. Serve sauce over steaks.

COOK'S FILE

Storage time: Cook this dish just before serving.

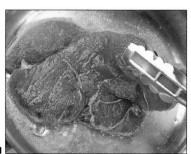

1

2

3

VEAL STEAKS WITH LEMON CREAM SAUCE

Preparation time: 10 minutes
+ 1 hour marinating
Cooking time: 10 minutes
Serves 4

4 veal steaks, about 130 g each
1 teaspoon finely grated
  lemon rind
¼ cup lemon juice
1 tablespoon olive oil
1 teaspoon ground black pepper
30 g butter
2 tablespoons olive oil, extra
½ cup cream
2 tablespoons chopped fresh
  parsley
1 tablespoon chopped fresh
  chives

➤ TRIM MEAT of excess fat and sinew. Flatten steaks to an even thickness. Nick edges to prevent curling.

1 Combine lemon rind, lemon juice, olive oil and pepper; add meat, coating well. Store in refrigerator, covered with plastic wrap, 1 hour or overnight, turning occasionally. Drain meat, reserving marinade.

2 Heat butter and extra oil in pan; add meat. Cook over high heat for 2 to 3 minutes on each side, turning once. Remove from pan; drain on absorbent paper, keep warm.

3 Add reserved marinade to pan with cream, parsley and chives. Bring to boil, reduce heat to a simmer, cook uncovered, for 2 minutes, pour over veal to serve.

COOK'S FILE

Storage time: Cook this dish just before serving.

Hint: Do not overcook the veal; it will quickly become dry.

VEAL MARSALA

Preparation time: 10 minutes
Cooking time: 6 minutes
Serves 4

4 veal steaks, about 185 g each
2 tablespoons plain flour
2 tablespoons oil
⅓ cup Marsala
⅓ cup chicken stock
1 tablespoon soy sauce
2 teaspoons plum conserve
1 spring onion, finely chopped

➤ TRIM MEAT of excess fat and sinew. Flatten steaks to an even thickness. Nick edges to prevent curling.

1 Spread the flour on a sheet of greaseproof paper. Toss veal lightly in flour; shake off excess.

2 Heat the oil in a heavy-based pan; add meat. Cook over a medium heat for 2 to 3 minutes each side, turning once. Remove meat from pan, drain on absorbent paper. Leave, covered with aluminium foil, in a warm place.

3 Add Marsala and stock to pan; bring to the boil. Boil 1 minute, uncovered, stirring constantly. Add sauce and conserve, stir until combined and heated through. Return veal steaks to pan, heat through in the sauce for 1 minute. Add spring onion; serve immediately.

COOK'S FILE

Storage time: Cook this dish just before serving.

Variation: Use a different fruit conserve for a sweeter or tarter flavour.

Hint: Marsala is a sweet, fortified wine. Substitute sweet sherry, if preferred. Marsala sauce can also be served over pan-fried pork.

1

2

3

VEAL CUTLETS

Preparation time: 20 minutes
+ 1 hour refrigeration
Cooking time: 12 minutes
Serves 6

12 veal cutlets, about
180 g each
6 thin slices Gruyère cheese
3 slices leg ham
¼ cup plain flour
¼ teaspoon ground black
pepper
2 eggs, lightly beaten
2 tablespoons milk
1½ cups/about 135 g packaged
breadcrumbs
¼ cup oil

➤ TRIM MEAT of excess fat and
sinew. Flatten the cutlets to an even

thickness. Nick the edges to prevent
meat curling.

1 Cut cheese slices slightly smaller
than cutlets (not including bone sec-
tion) leaving a 1 cm border. Cut ham
slices 1 cm larger than cheese.

2 Combine flour and pepper on a
sheet of greaseproof paper. Toss cutlets lightly in seasoned flour; shake off
excess. Place a cheese slice on each
cutlet, top with ham. Dust ham topping with seasoned flour.

3 Whisk eggs and milk lightly in a
small mixing bowl to combine. Place
breadcrumbs on a sheet of greaseproof
paper. Dip each cutlet into egg mixture. Coat with crumbs; shake off excess. Place cutlets on a foil-lined tray.
Store, covered, in the refrigerator for at
least 1 hour or overnight.

4 Heat the oil in heavy-based pan;
add cutlets a few at a time. Cook over
medium heat 2 to 3 minutes each side

or until tender, turning once. Remove
from pan; drain on absorbent paper.

COOK'S FILE

Storage time: Cook the cutlets just
before serving.

Hint: 'Resting' the cutlets once they
are crumbed helps to set the coating
before cooking. If you don't observe
this step, the coating will come away
from the cutlets and stick to the pan,
preventing an attractive, crisp finish.

LAMB'S LIVER AND BACON

Preparation time: 10 minutes
Cooking time: 30 minutes
Serves 6

1 lamb's liver, about 750 g
¼ cup cornflour
¼ teaspoon ground black
   pepper
6 rashers bacon
2 tablespoons oil
2 medium onions, finely
   sliced

1 beef stock cube, crumbled
1 cup boiling water

➤ WASH LIVER and slice thinly and evenly, discarding any veins or discoloured spots. Pat dry with absorbent paper.

1 Combine cornflour and pepper on a sheet of greaseproof paper. Toss the liver slices lightly in seasoned cornflour; shake off excess.

2 Cut bacon into large pieces. Cook in a heavy-based pan until crisp. Drain on absorbent paper. Add the oil to pan; add onion and fry gently until golden. Remove from pan with slotted spoon.

3 Cook liver quickly in small batches over medium heat until well browned; drain on absorbent paper.
Return liver, bacon and onion to pan. Dissolve the stock cube in boiling water; add stock gradually to pan. Stir over medium heat for 10 minutes or until liquid boils and thickens. Serve.

COOK'S FILE

Storage time: Cook this dish just before serving.
Hint: Many people find that liver has a rather strong flavour. Soaking it in milk for 30 minutes before cooking results in a milder taste.

1

2

3

LAMB SCHNITZELS WITH HERB AND LEMON BUTTER

Preparation time: 10 minutes
Cooking time: 4 to 6 minutes
Serves 4

4 lamb topside schnitzels
   or chump chops, about
   100 g each
1 tablespoon chilli oil

Herb and Lemon Butter
120 g butter
2 teaspoons finely grated
   lemon rind
1 tablespoon chopped fresh
   thyme
1 tablespoon chopped fresh
   parsley
1 tablespoon chopped fresh
   chives

➤ TRIM MEAT of excess fat and sinew.

1 Flatten meat to an even thickness. Nick edges to prevent curling.

2 Heat the oil in heavy-based pan; add the meat, cook over high heat for 2 minutes on each side, turning once for a rare result. For a medium result, cook a further 30 seconds on each side. For well done, cook a further 1 minute on each side. Serve topped with Herb and Lemon Butter.

3 To make the Herb and Lemon Butter: Place all ingredients in food processor bowl or blender, process for 30 seconds or until combined. Spoon onto a piece of aluminium foil, press into a log shape and wrap up. Refrigerate to firm; cut in 1 cm slices.

COOK'S FILE

Storage time: Cook meat just before serving. Herb and Lemon Butter can be made a day ahead and stored in the refrigerator.

Hint: For a quick and easy meal, prepare a double quantity of Herb and Lemon Butter. Use one serving now and store the rest in the freezer for up to 3 weeks. Thaw in refrigerator just before use.

Always nick edges of thin cuts of meat or meat will distort during cooking.

1

2

3

CRUSTY LAMB WITH GARLIC SAUCE

Preparation time: 20 minutes
+ 4 hours refrigeration
Cooking time: 10 minutes
Serves 6

6 Trim Lamb butterfly steaks,
  about 200 g each,
  or 12 lamb cutlets
1/3 cup plain flour
1/2 teaspoon ground black pepper
2 eggs, lightly beaten
1/2 cup/about 45 g packaged
  breadcrumbs
2 tablespoons crushed
  coriander seeds
1/3 cup olive oil

Garlic Sauce
6 cloves garlic, crushed
2 egg yolks, lightly beaten
2/3 cup olive oil
1 tablespoon lemon juice

➤ TRIM MEAT of any fat. Combine flour and pepper on a sheet of greaseproof paper. Toss meat lightly in seasoned flour; shake off excess.
1 Dip meat into beaten egg, a few pieces at a time. Coat with combined crumbs and seeds; press firmly, shake off excess. Arrange meat on foil-lined tray. Store in refrigerator, covered with plastic wrap, for 4 hours or overnight.
2 Heat oil in heavy-based pan; cook meat in batches over medium heat 2 to 3 minutes each side or until tender, turning once. Remove from pan, drain on absorbent paper. Serve with the Garlic Sauce.
3 To make Garlic Sauce: Place garlic and yolks in blender. Blend at high speed for 1 minute or until smooth. With the motor constantly operating, add oil a few drops at a time until it has all been added and the sauce is the consistency of mayonnaise. Stir in juice.

COOK'S FILE

Storage time: Cook meat just before serving.
Hint: Place the coriander seeds in a paper bag and crush them briefly with a rolling pin.
Garlic Sauce needs no cooking. Make just before serving because it may separate on standing.

1

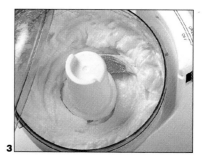

2

3

LAMB CUTLETS WITH REDCURRANT ORANGE GLAZE

Preparation time: 15 minutes
Cooking time: 15 minutes
Serves 4

12 lamb cutlets
2 tablespoons oil
2 cloves garlic, crushed

Redcurrant Orange Glaze
1 tablespoon thinly shredded
 orange rind
1 tablespoon thinly shredded
 fresh ginger

½ cup port
½ cup orange juice
½ cup redcurrant jelly
2 spring onions, finely chopped

➤ TRIM MEAT of excess fat and
sinew.
1 Heat the oil in a pan with the garlic;
add the cutlets, cook over high heat for
2 minutes on each side, turning once
for a rare result.
2 For medium and well done results,
reduce heat to medium. Cook a further
30 seconds on each side for medium.
Cook a further 1 minute on each side
for well done. Remove from pan; serve
with Redcurrant Orange Glaze
spooned over.

**3 To make Redcurrant Orange
Glaze:** Blanch orange rind and ginger
in boiling water for 1 minute, drain.
Combine in a small pan with port,
orange juice, redcurrant jelly and
spring onion, bring to boil. Reduce
heat to a simmer, cook, uncovered, for
5 minutes or until mixture has reduced
to 1 cup.

COOK'S FILE

Storage time: Cook this dish just
before serving.
Hint: A vegetable peeler is best for
removing rind from an orange. Peel
from top to bottom, making sure that
the rind is free of any white, bitter pith
which will spoil the taste of the dish.

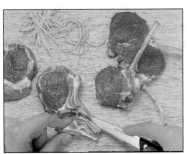

1

2

3

PORK STEAKS WITH GRAINY MUSTARD CREAM

Preparation time: 15 minutes
Cooking time: 12 minutes
Serves: 6

6 pork butterfly steaks, about
   200 g each, or 6 noisettes
3 tablespoons plain flour
½ teaspoon ground black
   pepper
¼ cup oil
1 medium onion, finely chopped
¾ cup orange juice
1 chicken stock cube, crumbled
1 teaspoon soy sauce
2 teaspoons seeded mustard
1 teaspoon cornflour
⅓ cup sour cream

➤ TRIM MEAT of excess fat and sinew.

1 Combine flour and pepper on a sheet of greaseproof paper. Coat steaks lightly in the seasoned flour; shake off excess.

2 Heat 2 tablespoons oil in a heavy-based pan; add meat. Cook over a medium heat 2 to 3 minutes each side or until tender, turning once. Remove from pan, drain on absorbent paper.

3 Heat remaining oil in pan. Add the onion, stir over medium heat 3 minutes or until soft. Add half the juice, stock cube, sauce and mustard, stir until combined. Blend cornflour with remaining juice until smooth; add to pan. Stir over low heat until sauce boils and thickens. Remove from heat; cool slightly. Add sour cream, stir until smooth. Return meat; heat through.

COOK'S FILE

Storage time: Cook this dish just before serving.

1

2

3

BRAISES & CASSEROLES

BEEF CURRY WITH POTATOES

Preparation time: 15 minutes
Cooking time: 1 hour 30 minutes
Serves 4

1 kg chuck steak
2 tablespoons oil
3/4 cup coconut cream
1/2 cup water
1 tablespoon tamarind sauce
500 g baby potatoes, halved

Spice Paste
2 medium onions, chopped
2 cloves garlic, chopped
2 teaspoons grated lemon rind
2 small red chillies, chopped
2 teaspoons ground
    coriander
2 teaspoons ground cumin
1 teaspoon turmeric
1/2 teaspoon ground cardamom
1 teaspoon garam masala

➤ TRIM MEAT of excess fat and sinew.

1 Cut meat evenly into 3 cm cubes. Heat oil in a heavy-based pan. Cook the meat quickly in small batches over medium-high heat until well browned; drain on absorbent paper.

2 Add Spice Paste to pan, stir over medium heat for 2 minutes. Return meat to pan with the coconut cream, water and tamarind sauce, bring to the boil. Reduce heat to a simmer, cook, covered, 30 minutes; stir occasionally.

3 Add the potato, cook for a further 30 minutes. Remove the lid, cook for another 30 minutes or until the meat is tender and almost all of the liquid has evaporated.

To make Spice Paste: Combine all ingredients in food processor bowl or blender, process 1 minute or until very finely chopped.

COOK'S FILE

Storage time: Curry will improve in flavour if made a day ahead. Store, covered, in refrigerator. Reheat just before serving. The curry can be frozen successfully for 1 month.

Variation: This is a mild-flavoured curry. If you prefer a little more heat, adjust the quantity of chillies to taste.

Hint: Chuck steak is ideal for recipes which require long, slow cooking. The meat becomes tender and flavoursome. Tamarind sauce has a distinctive sour taste; use lemon juice as a substitute.

CORNED BEEF WITH ONION SAUCE AND HORSERADISH CREAM

Preparation time: 5 minutes
Cooking time: 1 hour 30 minutes
Serves 6 to 8

1.5 kg piece corned silverside
1 tablespoon oil
1 tablespoon white vinegar
1 tablespoon soft brown sugar
4 whole cloves
4 whole black peppercorns
2 bay leaves
1 clove garlic, crushed
1 large sprig parsley
4 medium carrots
4 medium potatoes (800 g)
6 small onions

Onion Sauce
30 g butter
2 medium white onions,
    chopped
2 tablespoons plain flour
1⅓ cups milk

Horseradish Cream
3 tablespoons horseradish
    relish
1 tablespoon white vinegar
freshly ground black pepper,
    to taste
½ cup cream, whipped

➤ TRIM MEAT of excess fat and sinew.

1 Heat oil in a deep, heavy-based pan. Add meat and cook over medium-high heat, turning until well browned on all sides. Remove pan from heat; add vinegar, sugar, cloves, peppercorns, bay leaves, garlic and parsley.

2 Pour over enough water to cover. Return to heat. Reduce heat, cover pan and bring slowly to simmering point. Simmer for 30 minutes.

Cut the carrots and potatoes into large pieces; add to pan with onions and simmer, covered, for 1 hour or until tender. Remove vegetables with a slotted spoon and keep warm. Reserve ½ cup liquid for Onion Sauce.

Drain meat from pan, discarding the remaining liquid and spices. Slice meat and serve with vegetables, Onion Sauce and Horseradish Cream.

3 To make Onion Sauce: Heat the butter in a small pan. Add onion and cook gently for 10 minutes or until soft but not browned. Transfer onion to a bowl. Add flour to butter left in pan; stir over low heat for 2 minutes or until flour is lightly golden. Gradually add the milk and the ½ cup reserved liquid to pan; stir until the sauce boils and thickens. Boil for 1 minute; remove from heat and stir in the cooked onion. Season to taste.

4 To make Horseradish Cream: Combine all ingredients until smooth.

COOK'S FILE

Storage time: Leftover meat can be stored, covered, in the refrigerator for 2 days. Discard meat with sauce on it.
Hint: Silverside has a relatively coarse grain and a good flavour that develops well with slow cooking.

1

3

2

4

BRAISED OXTAIL

Preparation time: 15 minutes
Cooking time: 2 hours
Serves 6

¼ cup oil
16 small pieces oxtail, about
   1.5 kg
4 baby potatoes, cut in halves
1 large onion, chopped
2 medium carrots, chopped
250 g baby mushrooms
2 tablespoons plain flour
3 cups beef stock
1 teaspoon dried marjoram
   leaves
2 tablespoons Worcestershire
   sauce

➤ PREHEAT OVEN to moderate 180°C. Heat 2 tablespoons of the oil in a heavy-based pan.

1 Cook the oxtail quickly in small batches over medium-high heat until well browned; place in a deep casserole dish; add potato.

2 Heat the remaining oil in pan. Add onion and carrot, stir over medium heat 5 minutes. Place in casserole dish. Add the mushrooms to pan, stir over medium heat 5 minutes; stir in flour. Reduce heat to low, stir for 2 minutes.

3 Add stock gradually, stirring until the liquid boils and thickens. Add the marjoram and sauce. Pour mixture over the ingredients in casserole dish. Transfer to oven. Cook, covered, for 1 hour 30 minutes. Remove lid, stir; cook, uncovered, a further 30 minutes.

COOK'S FILE

Storage time: This dish can be frozen successfully for 1 month.
Hint: The gelatinous tendons that run the length of the oxtail soften during cooking, keeping the meat moist.

BEEF GOULASH WITH CARAWAY DUMPLINGS

Preparation time: 1 hour
Cooking time: 1 hour 15 minutes
Serves 6

1.5 kg round or topside steak
½ cup plain flour
¼ teaspoon ground black
 pepper
⅓ cup olive oil
1 clove garlic, crushed
2 medium onions, sliced
1 teaspoon ground sweet
 paprika
½ teaspoon ground cinnamon
⅓ cup red wine
½ cup beef stock
½ teaspoon dried mixed herbs
⅔ cup bottled chunky tomato
 sauce
3 large red capsicum

Caraway Dumplings
1½ cups self-raising flour
65 g butter
½ cup milk
1 teaspoon caraway seeds
1 tablespoon milk, extra

➤ PREHEAT OVEN to moderate 180°C.

1 Trim meat of excess fat and sinew, cut evenly into 3 cm cubes. Combine the flour and pepper on a sheet of greaseproof paper. Toss meat lightly in seasoned flour, shake off excess.

2 Heat 2 tablespoons of the oil in a heavy-based pan. Cook meat quickly in small batches over medium-high heat until well browned; drain on absorbent paper.

3 Heat remaining oil in pan. Add the garlic and onion, stir over a medium heat for 2 minutes or until soft.

4 Return meat to pan with spices, wine, stock, mixed herbs and tomato sauce; bring to the boil. Remove from heat, transfer to a deep casserole dish. Cook, covered, for 45 minutes. Remove from oven, remove lid. Increase oven temperature to hot 240°C.

5 Cut capsicum into halves lengthways; remove seeds. Place on a cold, greased oven tray, skin side up. Place under hot grill 10 minutes or until skin burns and blisters. Remove from grill, cool. Carefully peel off skins, discard. Cut capsicum into 2 cm wide strips. Arrange roasted capsicum over meat.

6 To make Caraway Dumplings: Place the flour and butter in a food processor bowl. Process for 10 seconds or until mixture is a fine, crumbly texture. Add the milk all at once, process 10 seconds or until a soft dough is formed. Turn the dough onto a lightly floured surface. Add the caraway seeds, knead 1 minute or until smooth. Press dough out to 1 cm thickness. Cut into 4 cm rounds using a fluted cutter. Top meat with Caraway Dumplings; brush with extra milk. Return to oven, cook, uncovered, for 15 minutes or until dumplings are puffed and golden.

COOK'S FILE

Storage time: Goulash can be cooked 1 day ahead without the dumplings. It can be frozen successfully, without the dumplings, for up to 1 month.

Variation: The dumplings can be flavoured with dried mixed herbs, ground sweet paprika or other herbs or spices of your choice instead of the caraway seeds. Use fresh herbs if preferred.

Thickly sliced potatoes can be added to the goulash at Step 4 instead of making dumplings. Alternatively, slice potatoes very thinly and evenly and place, overlapping, over the surface of the casserole. Dab with small pieces of butter. Cook until golden and crisp.

1

2

3

4

5

6

BEEF POT ROAST PROVENÇALE

Preparation time: 15 minutes
Cooking time: 2 hours 15 minutes
Serves 6

1 x 2 kg rolled beef brisket
2 tablespoons oil
3 cups beef stock
1 cup red wine
¼ cup brandy
2 medium onions, quartered
3 cloves garlic, crushed
3 medium tomatoes, peeled, seeded, chopped
2 bay leaves
¼ cup chopped fresh parsley

2 tablespoons fresh thyme leaves
12 pitted black olives
6 small carrots, thickly sliced
2 tablespoons plain flour
3 tablespoons water

➤ TRIM MEAT of excess fat and sinew.

1 Heat oil in a deep, heavy-based pan. Add meat, cook over medium-high heat until well browned on all sides, remove pan from heat.

2 Add stock to pan with the wine, brandy, onion, garlic, tomatoes, bay leaves, parsley and thyme. Reduce heat to low, return the pan to heat, covered. Bring slowly to simmering point, simmer for 1 hour 30 minutes.

3 Add olives and carrot, cook for a further 30 minutes. Remove meat from sauce. Leave in a warm place for about 10 minutes, covered with foil, before slicing. Blend flour with water to make a smooth paste. Add to sauce in pan, stir over medium heat until sauce thickens, cook 3 minutes. Pour over sliced meat to serve.

COOK'S FILE

Storage time: Cook this dish 1 day ahead. Any leftover meat can be refrigerated, covered, for 2 days.
Hint: Pot roasting a tougher cut of meat such as beef brisket gives a tender, juicy result. The juices that the meat exudes are very flavoursome and add depth to the sauce.

BRAISED BEEF WITH ONION AND RED WINE

Preparation time: 10 minutes
Cooking time: 2 hours
Serves 6

1 kg round or chuck steak
¼ cup plain flour
¼ teaspoon ground black pepper
1 tablespoon oil
15 g butter
12 small pickling onions

1 cup beef stock
1 cup red wine
2 tablespoons tomato paste
1 tablespoon French mustard
1 bay leaf
¼ teaspoon mixed dried herbs

➤ TRIM MEAT of excess fat and sinew.

1 Cut meat evenly into 3 cm pieces. Combine flour and pepper on grease-proof paper. Toss the meat lightly in seasoned flour; shake off excess.

2 Heat oil and butter in a heavy-based pan. Cook the meat quickly in small batches over medium-high heat until well browned; drain on absorbent paper.

3 Add the onions to pan and cook over medium-high heat until golden brown. Return meat to pan and stir in the stock, wine, tomato paste, mustard and herbs. Bring to the boil, reduce heat to a simmer. Cook, covered, for 1 hour 30 minutes or until meat is tender; stir occasionally.

COOK'S FILE

Storage time: This dish can be cooked 1 day ahead.

Beef Pot Roast Provençale (top), Braised Beef with Onion and Red Wine (bottom).

BEEF POT ROAST WITH EGGPLANT AND SWEET POTATO

Preparation time: 20 minutes
Cooking time: 1 hour 15 minutes
Serves 4

1 x 1 kg piece topside beef
2 tablespoons oil
1 cup beef stock
1 medium onion, sliced
1 clove garlic, crushed
4 large tomatoes, peeled, seeded, chopped
1 teaspoon ground cumin
1 teaspoon turmeric
1 teaspoon finely grated lemon rind
2 tablespoons lemon juice
1 medium eggplant, cut into 3 cm cubes
1 medium sweet potato, halved, cut into 1 cm slices
2 tablespoons plain flour
3 tablespoons water
1 tablespoon chopped fresh coriander

➤ TRIM MEAT of excess fat and sinew.

1 Heat oil in a deep, heavy-based pan, add whole piece of meat, cook over a medium-high heat until well browned on all sides.

2 Remove pan from heat, add stock, onion, garlic, tomato, cumin, turmeric, lemon rind and juice. Reduce heat to low, return pan to heat. Cover, bring slowly to simmering point, simmer for 45 minutes.

3 Add eggplant and sweet potato, cook a further 30 minutes, uncovered, until meat and vegetables are tender. Remove the meat from the sauce. Leave in a warm place, covered with foil, 10 minutes before slicing. Combine flour and water to make a smooth paste. Add to sauce with coriander, stir over medium heat until sauce boils and thickens, cook 3 minutes. Pour over sliced meat to serve.

COOK'S FILE

Storage time: Cook this dish just before serving.

Hint: Never allow a pot roast to boil. Long, slow cooking keeps the meat tender and moist.

1

2

3

BEEF BOURGUIGNONNE

Preparation time: 15 minutes
Cooking time: 1 hour 45 minutes
Serves 6

1 kg topside steak
100 g bacon pieces
30 g butter
2 tablespoons oil
18 baby onions
2 cloves garlic, crushed
3 tablespoons plain flour
2 cups red wine
3 cups beef stock
300 g small mushrooms

➤ TRIM MEAT of excess fat and sinew.

1 Cut meat evenly into 3 cm cubes. Trim bacon of excess fat and sinew, cut evenly into 1.5 cm cubes.

2 Heat butter and oil in heavy-based pan. Cook meat quickly in small batches over medium-high heat until browned; drain on absorbent paper.

3 Add bacon, onions and garlic to pan, cook, stirring, 2 minutes or until browned. Add flour, stir over low heat until flour is lightly golden. Gradually add wine and stock, stirring until mix-ture is smooth. Stir constantly over medium heat 2 minutes or until mix-ture boils and thickens.

4 Return meat to pan, reduce heat to a simmer. Cook, covered, for 1 hour 30 minutes or until meat is tender; stir occasionally. Add the mush-rooms, cook for 15 minutes.

COOK'S FILE

Storage time: This dish can be cooked 2 days ahead and refrigerated. Reheat gently.
Hint: Bacon pieces are available from delicatessens. Long, slow cooking gives this dish a rich, thick sauce.

IRISH STEW

Preparation time: 10 minutes
Cooking time: 2 hours 30 minutes
Serves 4

1 kg lamb neck chops
¼ cup plain flour
4 medium onions, sliced
2 cups water
8 medium potatoes (2 kg),
    quartered
¼ cup chopped fresh parsley

➤ PREHEAT OVEN to moderately slow 160°C.
1 Trim meat of excess fat and sinew. Toss in flour; shake off excess.
2 Place meat in a 2-litre ovenproof dish. Add onion and water, cover, cook for 1 hour 30 minutes.
3 Add potatoes, cook further 1 hour, covered, until meat and potatoes are tender. Add parsley, stir to combine.

COOK'S FILE

Storage time: Cook this dish just before serving.

Variation: The potatoes can also be sliced thickly and used to line the base of the dish. During the long, slow cooking, the potatoes will disintegrate, thickening and enriching the cooking liquid.
Add wide strips of bacon and chopped carrots for a more substantial meal.
Hint: Traditionally, Irish Stew is made from mutton which has a stronger flavour than lamb and benefits from lengthy cooking. Some butchers stock mutton on a regular basis or will order it in for you.

1

2

3

VEAL BIRDS IN TOMATO SAUCE

Preparation time: 12 minutes
Cooking time: 40 minutes
Serves 6

6 veal steaks, about 100 g each
12 thin slices prosciutto
1 cup grated mozzarella
    cheese
2 x 45 g cans anchovies in oil,
    drained
2 tablespoons plain flour
¼ teaspoon ground black
    pepper
2 tablespoons oil
⅓ cup dry white wine

⅓ cup chicken stock
½ cup bottled chunky tomato sauce
1 teaspoon capers
1 tablespoon chopped fresh parsley

➤ PREHEAT OVEN to moderate 180°C. Flatten steaks to an even thickness of about 3 mm.
1 Place 2 slices of prosciutto over each steak. Sprinkle 2 tablespoons cheese over the prosciutto and top with 3 anchovies.
2 Roll up the steaks and tie securely with string at regular intervals to retain their shape during cooking.
Combine flour and pepper on grease-proof paper. Toss the meat lightly in seasoned flour; shake off excess.

3 Heat oil in heavy-based pan. Cook meat quickly over medium heat until well browned all over. Arrange in a single layer over the base of a shallow casserole dish.
Add the wine, stock, sauce and capers to pan; bring to the boil. Pour over meat. Cover dish, transfer to oven, cook 35 minutes. Remove string just before serving. Serve sprinkled with chopped parsley.

COOK'S FILE

Storage time: Cook this dish just before serving.
Variation: Use sliced ham in place of the prosciutto.
Hint: Anchovies may be a little too salty for some palates. Soak in milk for 30 minutes if you prefer a milder taste.

1

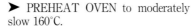

2

3

Irish Stew (top), Veal Birds in Tomato Sauce (bottom).

ALMOND AND COCONUT LAMB CURRY

Preparation time: 25 minutes
Cooking time: 40 minutes
Serves 4

8 lamb forequarter or chump
   chops, each about 140 g
¼ cup olive oil
1 medium onion, sliced
1 medium cooking apple, peeled
   and chopped
2 medium carrots, chopped
3 dried curry leaves

1 tablespoon fresh coriander
   leaves
½ teaspoon garam masala
½ teaspoon ground cumin
½ teaspoon turmeric
155 g can coconut cream
1 tablespoon ground almonds
¼ cup slivered almonds, toasted

➤ TRIM MEAT of excess fat and
sinew.
1 Cut chops evenly into 3 cm cubes;
discard bones.
2 Heat 2 tablespoons of the oil in a
heavy-based pan. Cook meat quickly
in small batches over medium-high
heat until well browned; drain on absorbent paper.
3 Heat remaining oil in pan. Add
onion, stir over medium heat 5 minutes
or until soft. Add meat with apple,
carrot, spices and coconut cream;
bring to boil. Reduce heat to a simmer,
cook, covered, 35 minutes or until meat
is tender. Stir in ground almonds just
before serving. Serve sprinkled with
toasted slivered almonds.

COOK'S FILE

Storage time: This can be cooked a
day ahead and refrigerated. It can be
frozen successfully for up to 1 month.

LAMB SHANKS WITH GARLIC

Preparation time: 20 minutes
Cooking time: 1 hour 15 minutes
Serves 6

6 large lamb shanks (knuckles)
freshly ground black pepper,
** to taste**
1 tablespoon oil
2 medium leeks, sliced
1 medium sprig rosemary
1 cup dry white wine
1 head garlic

➤ PREHEAT OVEN to moderate 180°C.

1 Season shanks with pepper. Heat oil in a heavy-based pan. Cook shanks quickly in batches over medium-high heat until well browned; drain on absorbent paper. Place in an ovenproof casserole.

2 Cook leek in pan until tender. Add to casserole with rosemary and wine.

3 Cut whole garlic through the centre horizontally. Brush cut surfaces with a little oil. Place cut side up in casserole, but not covered by liquid. Cover pan and bake for 1 hour. Remove lid and cook a further 15 minutes. Discard rosemary before serving. Serve with steamed vegetables and crusty bread on which to spread the roasted garlic.

COOK'S FILE

Storage time: Cook this dish just before serving.

Hint: Lamb should be soft and falling from the bones.

Don't be alarmed by the amount of garlic used in this dish. Roasted garlic has a milder flavour than raw or fried garlic. The longer it is cooked, the milder and softer it becomes.

CASSOULET

Preparation time: 20 minutes
+ overnight soaking
Cooking time: 4 hours
Serves 6

500 g dried haricot beans
1½ litres beef stock
500 g pork spareribs
250 g cubed lamb
2 tablespoons oil
250 g garlic or spiced sausage
125 g piece bacon, cut into
　cubes
2 medium onions, chopped
2 medium carrots, chopped
2 cloves garlic, crushed
1 bay leaf
1 sprig parsley
1 sprig thyme

6 whole black peppercorns
2 cups/about 90 g coarse
　breadcrumbs
60 g firm butter, grated

➤ SOAK BEANS overnight in water.
1 Drain and place in a large pan with stock. Bring slowly to boiling point, reduce heat to a simmer and cook for 1 hour until tender. Drain; retain liquid.
2 Trim excess fat and sinew from meats. Heat oil in pan and brown meats, sausage and bacon in several batches. Remove and drain on absorbent paper. Add onion, carrot and garlic to pan and brown well.
3 Preheat the oven to moderately slow 160°C. Layer meats, drained beans and vegetables in a large ovenproof casserole.
Tie herbs and peppercorns together in a small piece of muslin and add to

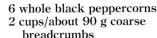

dish. Pour over liquid from beans, cover dish and bake for 2 hours.
4 Remove the herb bag and discard. Combine breadcrumbs and butter and sprinkle over top of casserole. Return to oven and cook for 30 minutes or until crust is golden and crisp.

COOK'S FILE

Storage time: Cook 2 days ahead without the breadcrumbs and butter. Reheat with the topping ingredients.

BRAISED PORK MEDALLIONS WITH PRUNES

Preparation time: 15 minutes
Cooking time: 30 minutes
Serves 4

4 pork loin medallions, about
    175 g each
2 cups chicken stock
2 tablespoons oil
1 large onion, cut into wedges
2 cloves garlic, crushed
1 tablespoon fresh thyme leaves

1 large tomato, peeled, seeded,
    finely chopped
1/2 cup cream
16 pitted prunes

➤ TRIM MEAT of excess fat and
sinew.
1 Shape into rounds by securing a
length of string around the medallions.
Tie with a bow for easy removal.
Place the stock in medium pan, bring
to boil. Reduce heat to a simmer, cook,
uncovered, for 5 minutes or until
reduced to ¾ cup.
2 Heat oil in a heavy-based pan, add
meat. Cook over high heat 2 minutes

each side to seal, turning once; drain
on absorbent paper.
3 Add the onion and garlic to pan,
stir 2 minutes. Return meat to pan
with thyme, tomato and stock, reduce
heat to low. Cover pan, bring slowly to
simmering point, simmer 10 minutes
or until meat is tender, turning once.
Add cream and prunes, simmer for a
further 5 minutes.

COOK'S FILE

Storage time: Cook this dish just
before serving.
Hint: Use a firm, well ripened tomato
for this recipe.

1

2

3

FAMILY FARE

FAMILY MEAT PIE

Preparation time: 15 minutes
Cooking time: 40 minutes
Serves 4 to 6

750 g minced beef
1 tablespoon oil
1 medium onion, chopped
100 g button mushrooms, sliced
1 cup beef stock
2 tablespoons tomato paste
2 tablespoons plain flour
2 sheets frozen shortcrust
   pastry, thawed
1 sheet frozen puff pastry,
   thawed
1 egg, lightly beaten

➤ PREHEAT OVEN to very hot 240°C.

1 Heat oil in a heavy-based pan; add onion and mince. Cook over medium-high heat until meat is well browned and almost all liquid has evaporated. Use a fork to break up any lumps.

2 Add the mushrooms, stock and tomato paste. Reduce heat, simmer, uncovered, for 15 minutes. Mix the flour with a little cold water to make a smooth paste. Stir into meat, bring to the boil and cook until sauce has thickened. Cool.

3 Line a 23 cm pie plate with short-crust pastry, overlapping the sheets if necessary. Fill with cold meat mixture. Moisten edges with water, cover with puff pastry and press edges together to seal. Trim excess pastry and use to decorate top, if desired.

4 Brush top with beaten egg and make a few steam holes. Place dish on a baking tray in oven; cook 10 minutes. Reduce oven temperature to moderate 180°C and bake for 30 minutes or until pastry is golden.

COOK'S FILE

Storage time: Cook this dish just before serving.
Variation: To make individual pies, cut circles from the pastry to fit small pie plates, using a plate as a guide.

BAKED PASTA AND MINCE

Preparation time: 15 minutes
Cooking time: 2 hours
Serves 8

2 tablespoons olive oil
1 large onion, chopped
1 kg minced beef
¼ cup red wine
700 mL jar bottled chunky
   tomato sauce
2 chicken stock cubes, crumbled
2 tablespoons finely chopped
   fresh parsley
500 g tubular spaghetti
2 egg whites, lightly beaten
2 tablespoons packaged
   breadcrumbs

Cheese Sauce
2 tablespoons butter
2 tablespoons plain flour
2½ cups milk
2 egg yolks, lightly beaten
1 cup/100 g grated Cheddar
   cheese

➤ PREHEAT OVEN to moderate 180°C.

1 Heat oil in heavy-based pan; add onion. Cook over a medium heat for 2 minutes or until soft. Add mince, stir over high heat until well browned and almost all liquid has evaporated.

2 Add the wine, sauce and stock cubes, bring to the boil. Reduce to a simmer and cook, covered, for 1 hour, stirring occasionally. Remove from heat; add parsley, cool.

3 Bring pan of water to a rapid boil; add pasta and cook until just tender. Drain, rinse under cold water, drain well. Combine pasta with egg whites. Place half the spaghetti over base of greased, deep, ovenproof dish. Cover with mince mixture.

4 Combine remaining spaghetti with Cheese Sauce and spread over mince. Sprinkle with breadcrumbs. Bake for 45 minutes or until lightly golden.

To make Cheese Sauce: Heat the butter in a medium pan; add flour. Stir over low heat 2 minutes or until flour mixture is lightly golden. Add milk gradually to pan, stirring until mixture is smooth. Stir constantly over a medium heat for 5 minutes or until mixture boils and thickens; boil for 1 minute; remove from heat. Cool slightly; stir in yolks and cheese.

COOK'S FILE

Storage time: Cook this dish just before serving. It freezes successfully for up to 2 weeks.

1

2

3

4

BEEF MINCE PIZZA

Preparation time: 10 minutes
Cooking time: 40 minutes
Serves 4 to 6

500 g lean minced beef
1 medium onion, finely chopped
1 clove garlic, crushed
1 teaspoon mixed dried herbs
¼ cup tomato paste
1 cup grated mozzarella cheese
100 g mushrooms, sliced
1 small red capsicum, cut
  into strips
1 small green capsicum, cut
  into strips
20 pitted black olives, chopped

➤ PREHEAT OVEN to moderate 180°C.

1 Combine mince, onion, garlic and herbs. Press out mixture onto a 28 cm pizza tray or into a thin round on a baking tray.

2 Top with the tomato paste, cheese, mushrooms, capsicum and olives.

Place on a larger tray to catch any overflowing oil.

3 Cover with aluminium foil and cook for 30 minutes, pouring off excess oil regularly. Remove from oven, discard aluminium foil; return to oven and cook for 10 minutes. Serve with salad.

COOK'S FILE

Storage time: The beef pizza base can be cooked 1 day ahead; refrigerate. Freeze meat base for up to 2 months.
Variation: Add other toppings such as sliced tomato, pineapple or bacon.

1

2

3

STEAK AND KIDNEY PUDDING

Preparation time: 30 minutes
Cooking time: 4 hours
Serves 4

500 g round or rump steak
200 g lamb kidneys
2 tablespoons plain flour
30 g butter
1 tablespoon oil
1 medium onion, sliced
1 clove garlic, crushed
125 g button mushrooms,
   quartered
½ cup red wine
1 cup beef stock
2 tablespoons chopped
   fresh parsley
1 bay leaf

Suet Pastry
1½ cups self-raising flour
90 g suet, skinned, finely grated
½ cup water, approximately

➤ TRIM MEAT of excess fat and sinew.

1 Cut meat evenly into 3 cm cubes. Peel skin from kidneys, cut kidneys into quarters, trim any fat or sinew. Toss meat and kidneys in flour.

2 Heat the butter and oil in a heavy-based pan. Add the onion and garlic, stirring until soft; remove. Add the meat and kidneys in small batches, cooking them quickly over a medium-high heat until well browned; drain on absorbent paper.

3 Return the onion, garlic, meat and kidneys to pan with mushrooms, wine, stock, parsley and bay leaf; bring to the boil. Reduce heat to a simmer, cook, covered, for 1 hour or until the meat is tender, stirring occasionally; allow mixture to cool.

4 **To make Suet Pastry:** Sift flour into a bowl, stir in the grated suet. Add sufficient water to mix to a firm dough. Knead on a lightly floured surface until smooth. Roll two-thirds of suet pastry to fit the base and sides of an 8-cup pudding basin; brush the top edge with water.

5 Spoon meat filling into pastry. Roll remaining pastry to cover basin, press edges of pastry firmly together to seal. Grease a sheet of greaseproof paper large enough to cover the top of the basin plus about 5 cm all round. Place a sheet of foil on top of pudding.

6 Place foil over pudding, secure tightly with string. Place basin in a large pan. Add enough water to come halfway up sides of basin. Bring to boil, reduce heat to a simmer, cook, covered, 3 hours. Turn out, cut into wedges to serve.

COOK'S FILE

Storage time: Cook this dish just before serving.

Hint: Adding suet to a steamed pudding pastry produces a pastry that is rich in flavour and has a slightly crisp texture. Suet can be purchased from your butcher.

Check the water level in the saucepan occasionally during cooking. Replenish with boiling water as necessary to prevent the pan boiling dry.

Calf's (veal) kidney is the best for grilling or pan-frying; lamb kidneys are a little less rich in flavour and can be used in the same way, as well as in steamed meat puddings. Pigs' kidneys have a strong flavour and are well suited to braising and stewing; they yield a deliciously rich sauce.

Kidneys can be refrigerated for 1 day before use. Discard any which have a strong smell of ammonia; this indicates that they are stale or have not been properly handled.

1

2

3

4

5

6

PIQUANT COUNTRY BEEF WITH HERB SCONES

Preparation time: 30 minutes
Cooking time: 2 hours 10 minutes
Serves 4

1 kg chuck steak
¼ cup plain flour
3 tablespoons oil
4 medium onions, roughly
  chopped
2 cloves garlic, crushed
⅓ cup plum jam
⅓ cup brown vinegar
1 cup beef stock
2 teaspoons sweet chilli sauce

Herb Scones
2 cups self-raising flour
30 g butter
2 tablespoons chopped
  fresh chives
2 tablespoons chopped fresh
  parsley
¾ cup milk

➤ PREHEAT OVEN to moderate 180°C. Trim meat of excess fat and sinew. Cut meat evenly into 3 cm cubes. Toss in flour, shaking off the excess.

1 Heat 2 tablespoons oil in a heavy-based pan. Cook meat quickly, in small batches, over medium-high heat until well browned; drain on absorbent paper.

2 Heat the remaining oil in pan, add onion and garlic and cook, stirring, for 3 minutes or until soft. Combine onion mixture and meat in a large bowl.

3 Add the plum jam, vinegar, stock, and chilli sauce, mix well. Transfer mixture to an ovenproof dish. Cover and bake for 1 hour 30 minutes or until the meat is tender.

4 Uncover dish, turn oven up to hot 240°C. Place Herb Scones on top of meat, bake, uncovered, for 30 minutes or until scones are golden brown.

To make Herb Scones: Sift flour into a bowl, rub in butter until mixture resembles fine breadcrumbs. Stir in chives and parsley. Add milk, stir until just combined. Turn onto a lightly floured surface, knead until smooth.

Press dough out to a 4 cm thick round; cut into rounds with a 5 cm cutter.

COOK'S FILE

Storage time: The casserole can be cooked 2 days ahead without the scones and refrigerated. It can be frozen successfully for up to 2 weeks. Reheat, adding scones.

Variation: Use 1 tablespoon chopped fresh rosemary or basil in place of the chives or parsley.

FETTUCCINE BOLOGNESE

Preparation time: 10 minutes
Cooking time: 1 hour 40 minutes
Serves 6

2 tablespoons oil
2 medium onions,
    chopped
2 cloves garlic, crushed
500 g minced beef
250 g small mushrooms,
    chopped
1 x 440 g can tomatoes with
    their liquid, crushed
½ cup tomato paste
2 tablespoons chopped
    fresh basil
1 tablespoon chopped fresh
    oregano
1 litre water
500 g dried fettuccine

➤ HEAT OIL in heavy-based pan, add the onion, stir over medium heat for 3 minutes or until soft. Add garlic, stir 1 minute.

1 Add the meat, cook over a high heat for 5 minutes until well browned and all the liquid has evaporated. Use a fork to break up any lumps of mince as it cooks.

2 Add the mushrooms, crushed tomatoes and their liquid, the tomato paste, basil, oregano and water. Bring to the boil, reduce heat to a simmer. Cook, uncovered, for 1 hour 30 minutes, or until the sauce has reduced and thickened.

3 Bring a large pan of water to the boil. Add fettuccine, cook until just tender, drain. Serve with meat sauce.

COOK'S FILE

Storage time: Bolognese Sauce can be frozen for up to 2 months.
Variation: Serve the sauce with any pasta shape of your choice. Use other fresh herbs of your choice.

CORNISH PASTIES

Preparation time: 45 minutes
Cooking time: 30 minutes
Makes 8

250 g blade or chuck steak
1 medium potato
1 medium carrot
1 medium onion
2 tablespoons tomato sauce
2 tablespoons fruit chutney
2 teaspoons Worcestershire
   sauce

Pastry
2 cups plain flour
125 g butter
1 egg, separated
3 tablespoons water

➤ PREHEAT OVEN to hot 240°C.
1 Trim meat of excess fat and sinew, chop meat finely. Coarsely grate the potato, carrot and onion, drain on absorbent paper. Combine vegetables in a bowl with the meat, tomato sauce, chutney and Worcestershire sauce.

2 To make Pastry: Sift flour into a bowl, rub in butter until the mixture resembles fine breadcrumbs. Stir in egg yolk and enough water to mix to a firm dough. Turn onto a lightly floured surface, knead until smooth. Roll the dough out thinly, cut into 8 x 15 cm rounds.

3 Divide the meat mixture between pastry rounds, brush edges of pastry with a little beaten egg white. Fold pastry over to enclose filling, press edges together.

4 With join at the top, pinch a frill along the edge. Brush pasties with beaten egg white, place on lightly greased baking tray. Bake 15 minutes. Reduce heat to moderate 180°C, bake further 15 minutes or until brown.
Serve with tomato sauce or chutney.

COOK'S FILE

Storage time: Cornish Pasties can be made up to 2 days ahead and refrigerated. Reheat in a moderate 180°C oven for 15 minutes.
Hint: For pastry, place flour and butter in processor bowl, process 20 seconds. Add the egg yolk and water. Using pulse action, process 5 seconds or until ingredients are just combined.

1

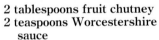

2

3

4

CHILLI BEEF AND BEANS

Preparation time: 6 minutes
Cooking time: 20 minutes
Serves 4

500 g rump steak
2 tablespoons oil
2 cloves garlic, crushed
1 x 35 g sachet Taco Seasoning
  Mix
1 tablespoon tomato paste

¾ cup water
1 tablespoon sweet chilli sauce
1 x 440 g can red kidney beans,
  rinsed, drained

➤ TRIM MEAT of excess fat and sinew.

1 Cut meat evenly into very small pieces about 3 mm thick.

2 Heat oil in heavy-based pan. Cook meat quickly in small batches over a high heat until well browned; reduce heat to medium.

3 Add garlic, seasoning mix, paste, water and sauce to pan; bring to the boil. Reduce heat to a simmer. Cook, covered, for 15 minutes, stirring the mixture occasionally. Add beans, cook, covered, for 5 minutes.

Serve chilli beef and beans in taco shells with shredded lettuce, mashed avocado and sour cream, if desired.

COOK'S FILE

Storage time: Meat can be cooked a day ahead and gently reheated.

SHEPHERD'S PIE

Preparation time: 15 minutes
Cooking time: 1 hour 15 minutes
Serves 4 to 6

2 tablespoons oil
1 medium onion, chopped
1 clove garlic, crushed
750 g minced lamb
250 g button mushrooms, sliced
⅓ cup tomato paste
1 tablespoon Worcestershire
   sauce
3 tablespoons chopped fresh
   parsley
2 tablespoons dry sherry
2 tablespoons cornflour
1½ cups beef stock

Topping
4 large potatoes
   (about 1 kg), chopped
350 g pumpkin, chopped
30 g butter
1 egg, lightly beaten

➤ PREHEAT OVEN to moderate 180°C.

1 Heat oil in heavy-based pan. Add onion and garlic, cook, stirring, until soft. Add mince, cook over high heat for 5 minutes or until well browned and all the liquid has evaporated. Use a fork to break up any lumps of mince as it cooks.

2 Add the mushrooms, tomato paste, Worcestershire sauce, parsley and sherry, stirring until combined. Combine cornflour with stock until smooth.

Add to pan, stir over a medium heat for 3 minutes or until the mixture boils. Reduce heat to a simmer. Cook, covered, 25 minutes; stir occasionally.

3 Spoon mixture into a 2-litre oven-proof dish or a 23 cm pie plate. Spread with Topping. Bake for 45 minutes or until brown.

To make Topping: Cook potato and pumpkin in boiling water 10 minutes or until tender; drain. Place potato and pumpkin in a bowl, add butter and egg, mash until smooth.

COOK'S FILE

Storage time: Cook this dish just before serving. It freezes successfully for up to 1 month.

Variation: Use cooked minced beef in place of lamb to make Cottage Pie.

LAMB AND FILO PIE

Preparation time: 5 minutes
Cooking time: 50 minutes
Serves 6

2 tablespoons oil
2 medium onions, chopped
1 kg minced lamb
¼ cup chopped fresh parsley
2 tablespoons chopped fresh
  mint
1 teaspoon ground cinnamon
½ cup pine nuts
1 x 375 g packet filo pastry
250 g unsalted butter, melted

➤ HEAT OIL in a heavy-based pan; add onion and mince.

1 Cook over a medium-high heat for 10 minutes or until well browned and all the liquid has evaporated. Use a fork to break up any lumps of mince as it cooks. Stir in parsley, mint, cinnamon and pine nuts; mix well.

2 Preheat oven to moderate 180°C. Lightly grease a 33 x 23 cm ovenproof dish with butter or oil. Work with 2 sheets of filo at a time, keeping the remainder covered with a clean, damp tea-towel to prevent them drying out. Brush the top sheet of the first 2 sheets with melted butter. Place a further 2 pastry sheets on top and again brush with butter. Line the baking dish with these 4 sheets; do not trim the excess.

3 Spread a quarter of the lamb mixture over the pastry sheets. Continue buttering and layering 4 pastry sheets and meat alternately, finishing with 2 sheets of pastry. Fold overhanging ends over onto the top.

Bake for 40 minutes or until pastry is crisp and golden.

COOK'S FILE

Storage time: Cook this dish just before serving.

Hint: Filo very quickly becomes dry and brittle if exposed to the air.

LAMB AND EGGPLANT BAKE

Preparation time: 30 minutes
Cooking time: 1 hour
Serves 6 to 8

3 large eggplant, cut into
    rounds 4 mm thick
2 tablespoons salt
½ cup olive oil
1 kg minced lamb
410 g can tomatoes, with their
    liquid, crushed
¼ cup tomato paste
2 cloves garlic, crushed
2 teaspoons dried oregano
    leaves
½ teaspoon ground cinnamon

Potato Topping
4 large potatoes (about 1 kg),
    chopped

2 eggs, lightly beaten
¼ cup milk
¼ teaspoon ground cinnamon
½ cup freshly grated Parmesan
    cheese

➤ PREHEAT OVEN to moderate 180°C.

1 Coat eggplant rounds with salt. Place in colander for 1 hour to draw out the bitter juices. Rinse with cold water; squeeze dry.

2 Heat 3 tablespoons oil in a heavy-based pan. Cook eggplant a few pieces at a time over medium heat until well browned, adding more oil when necessary; drain on absorbent paper.

3 Add mince to pan with any remaining oil. Cook over a medium heat for 10 minutes or until well browned and almost all liquid has evaporated.

4 Add the tomatoes, paste, garlic, oregano and cinnamon; bring to the boil. Reduce heat to a simmer, cook, uncovered, 10 minutes; stir occasionally.

5 Arrange eggplant over base of deep, ovenproof dish; spread with mince mixture. Spread Potato Topping over mince; swirl the surface with a fork, to decorate. Bake 40 minutes or until lightly golden.

106

6 To make Potato Topping: Cook the potato in a large pan of boiling water for 10 minutes or until tender. Drain; cool. Using a fork, mash in a large bowl. Add the eggs, milk, cinnamon and cheese, beating with a fork to thoroughly combine.

COOK'S FILE

Storage time: This can be assembled 4 hours ahead and refrigerated. Bring to room temperature and cook.
Variation: A topping of cooked mashed sweet potato and potato can be used in place of just the potato. Omit the Parmesan cheese. Sprinkle the top of the Eggplant Bake with a little grated Cheddar cheese a few minutes before the end of the cooking time. Cheese should be just melted. Serve at once.

HOME-STYLE LAMB PIE

Preparation time: 40 minutes
Cooking time: 55 minutes
Serves 4 to 6

1 kg boned leg lamb
1 tablespoon olive oil
20 g butter
1 medium onion, chopped
2 tablespoons plain flour
1½ cups tomato juice
¼ cup port
1 tablespoon red wine vinegar
2 tablespoons tomato paste
1 teaspoon ground oregano
1 medium carrot, halved, cut
   into 1 cm thick slices
1 medium parsnip, halved, cut
   into 1 cm thick slices
1 medium leek, thinly sliced
1 x 375 g packet puff pastry
1 egg, lightly beaten

➤ TRIM MEAT of excess fat and sinew. Cut meat into 1 cm cubes.

1 Heat oil and butter in large heavy-based pan. Add onion, cook, stirring until soft. Remove from pan, drain on absorbent paper. Cook meat in small batches over a medium high heat until well browned; drain on absorbent paper. Add flour to pan, cook, stirring, 1 minute, stir in tomato juice, port, vinegar, tomato paste and oregano. Stir continuously until mixture boils and thickens.

2 Return onion and meat to pan with vegetables. Bring to boil, reduce heat, simmer, uncovered, for 15 minutes. Remove from heat, cool.

Preheat oven to moderate 180°C. Roll two thirds of the puff pastry large enough to line base and sides of deep 20 cm cake tin. Fill with meat mixture.

3 Roll remaining pastry to fit over pie. Moisten edges with egg, trim pastry leaving a 1 cm overlapping border. Twist edges together. Brush pie with egg; make 3 cuts in top to allow steam to escape. Bake 40 minutes or until pastry is golden.

GOURMET MEATLOAF

Preparation time: 20 minutes
Cooking time: 1 hour 15 minutes
Serves 6

500 g pork and veal mince
250 g sausage mince
1½ cups/about 65 g fresh white
    breadcrumbs
1 small green capsicum,
    chopped
1 medium onion, finely chopped
2 cloves garlic, crushed
½ cup bottled chunky
    tomato sauce
½ cup fruit chutney
1 egg, lightly beaten
½ cup chopped dried apricots

1 tablespoon green
    peppercorns, drained,
    chopped
2 tablespoons chopped fresh
    mint
2 teaspoons ground sweet
    paprika
1 tablespoon toasted sesame
    seeds

Tomato Cream Sauce
1½ cups bottled chunky
    tomato sauce
½ cup cream
3 teaspoons seeded mustard

➤ GREASE 23 x 13 cm loaf pan.
Preheat oven to moderate 180°C.
1 Combine pork and veal mince and
sausage mince in a bowl. Add the

breadcrumbs, capsicum, onion, garlic,
tomato sauce, chutney, egg, apricots,
peppercorns, mint and paprika, mix
until thoroughly combined.
2 Press into prepared loaf pan, bake,
uncovered, 1 hour 15 minutes. Pour off
juices. Turn out meatloaf, sprinkle
with sesame seeds. Serve sliced with
Tomato Cream Sauce.
**3 To make the Tomato Cream
Sauce:** Combine all the ingredients in
pan. Bring to the boil. Reduce heat to
a simmer, cook for 3 minutes, stirring
occasionally.

COOK'S FILE

Storage time: Cook meatloaf just
before serving. It freezes successfully
for up to 1 month.
Hint: Also good cold in sandwiches.

PORK MEATBALLS WITH CREAMY MUSHROOM SAUCE

Preparation time: 5 minutes
Cooking time: 25 minutes
Serves 4 to 6

375 g minced pork
2 spring onions, chopped
1 tablespoon chopped fresh
  parsley
1 tablespoon lemon juice
1 teaspoon finely grated lemon
  rind
¼ teaspoon ground black
  pepper
1 egg, lightly beaten
¼ cup plain flour
½ cup oil
350 g fettuccine

Mushroom Sauce
15 g butter
1 clove garlic, crushed
50 g button mushrooms, sliced
2 tablespoons pine nuts
½ teaspoon balsamic vinegar
1¼ cups cream
¼ cup freshly grated Parmesan
  cheese

➤ MIX PORK, onion, parsley, lemon juice, rind and pepper together.
1 Roll level tablespoonfuls into balls; dip into egg and coat with flour.
2 Heat oil in a large pan. Add meatballs, cook in batches for 20 minutes or until cooked. Remove from pan and drain on absorbent paper. Keep warm. Bring a large pan of boiling, salted water to the boil. Add fettuccine, cook until just tender. Drain fettuccine and serve immediately with meatballs and Mushroom Sauce.
3 To make Mushroom Sauce: Heat the butter in pan; add the garlic, mushrooms and pine nuts and cook over high heat until mushrooms have browned. Add vinegar and cook until evaporated. Stir in cream and cheese and simmer for 5 minutes or until sauce has thickened slightly.

COOK'S FILE

Storage time: Meatballs can be made 2 days in advance; store, covered, in the refrigerator. They can be frozen successfully for up to 1 month.

INDEX

USEFUL INFORMATION

All our recipes are thoroughly tested in our test kitchen. Standard metric measuring cups and spoons approved by Standards Australia are used in the development of our recipes. All cup and spoon measurements are level. We have used eggs with an average weight of 60 g each in all recipes. Can sizes vary from manufacturer to manufacturer and between countries; use the can size closest to the one suggested in the recipe.

Australian Metric Cup and Spoon Measures

For dry ingredients the standard set of metric measuring cups consists of 1 cup, ½ cup, ⅓ cup and ¼ cup sizes.

For measuring liquids, a transparent, graduated measuring jug is available in either a 250 mL cup or a 1 litre jug.

The basic set of metric spoons, used to measure both dry and liquid ingredients, is made up of 1 tablespoon, 1 teaspoon, ½ teaspoon and ¼ teaspoon.

Note: Australian tablespoon equals 20 mL. British, US and NZ tablespoons equal 15 mL for use in liquid measuring. The teaspoon has a 5 mL capacity and is the same for Australian, British and American markets.

Weights

Metric		Imperial
120 g	=	4 oz
180 g	=	6 oz
240 g	=	8 oz
300 g	=	10 oz
360 g	=	12 oz
420 g	=	14 oz
480 g	=	1 lb
720 g	=	1 lb 8 oz
1 kg	=	2 lb 2 oz
1.4 kg	=	3 lb
1.9 kg	=	4 lb
2.4 kg	=	5 lb

Measures

1 cm	=	½ in
2.5 cm	=	1 in
25 cm	=	10 in
30 cm	=	12 in

Oven Temperatures

Electric	C	F
Very Slow	120	250
Slow	150	300
Mod Slow	160	325
Moderate	180	350
Mod Hot	210	425
Hot	240	475
Very Hot	260	525
Gas	**C**	**F**
Very Slow	120	250
Slow	150	300
Mod Slow	160	325
Moderate	180	350
Mod Hot	190	375
Hot	200	400
Very Hot	230	450

British and American Cup and Spoon Conversion

Australian	British/American
1 tablespoon	3 teaspoons
2 tablespoons	¼ cup
¼ cup	⅓ cup
⅓ cup	½ cup
½ cup	⅔ cup
⅔ cup	¾ cup
¾ cup	1 cup
1 cup	1¼ cups

Glossary

Australian	British/American	Australian	British/American
Unsalted Butter	Unsalted /Sweet Butter	Eggplant	Aubergine
125 g butter	125 g butter/1 stick of butter	Plain Flour	Plain Flour/All-Purpose
Bicarbonate of Soda	Bicarbonate of Soda/ Baking Soda	Self-Raising Flour	Self-Raising/Self-Rising Flour
Caster Sugar	Castor Sugar/Superfine Sugar	Sultanas	Golden Raisins/Seedless White Raisins
Cornflour	Cornflour/Cornstarch		
Capsicum	Sweet Pepper	Zucchini	Courgettes

Manager Food Publications: Jo Anne Calabria
Recipe Origination: Wendy Berecry, Christine Sheppard, Voula Mantzouridis
Home Economists – Testing and Step-by-step Photography: Kerrie Ray, Tracy Rutherford, Melanie McDermont
Food Stylist: Carolyn Fienberg

Food Stylist's Assistant: Jo Forrest
Step-By-Step Photography: Reg Morrison
Photography: Jon Bader
Managing Editor: Lynn Humphries
Design and Art Direction: Lena Lowe

Publisher: Anne Wilson
Publishing Manager: Mark Newman
Production Manager: Catie Ziller

Marketing Manager: Mark Smith
National Sales Manager: Keith Watson
National Library of Australia Cataloguing-in-Publication-Data
Favourite meat recipes step-by-step
Includes index.
ISBN 0 86411 307 2.
1. Cookery (Meat)
641.66